Don't Be That Girl

The American Dream is Not your Reality

Aisha Mene Stokes

Don't Be That Girl

The American Dream is Not your Reality

Design and Production by Adell& Co.

ISBN: 978-0-578-44284-6

United States:

www.singlewomanadvocate.com

Dedicated to my beautiful daughter Ngozi Obiaku Baier.

Always be authentic in who you are.

"Ladies, it's time we stop living the cookie cutter lifestyle and walk in our own purpose."

Author Aisha M. Stokes

TABLE OF CONTENTS

Ngozi Obiaku Baier,

It is so important to always be confident in whatever you do. A confident woman is secure within herself. She is decisive and goes after what she wants. Be the girl who has options. Walk in your power by deleting and blocking people from your life who destroy your energy and dim your light. Be authentic because you are enough! That phrase is so powerful, it bares repeating: YOU ARE ENOUGH! You don't have to accept a mediocre lifestyle or mediocre relationships. Go after your dreams and do not let anyone stop you. Do not let anyone bring your self-esteem down. Understand that you are in charge of your happiness, so decide to be happy. Spend time alone and know thyself. The company you keep is a direct reflection of you, so do yourself a favor and be very picky when choosing friends. It's okay to have high standards and want nothing but the best for yourself. You deserve the best. I want you to respect your body, respect your mind, and understand that you are nobody's possession. You are no one's second choice.

If you ever decide to have children make sure it's on your terms. Make sure you've experienced everything you wanted to experience in life. Never live your life wishing you could have done it all over. No regrets! Be a lady at all times: take care of your body, never go outside with a hair bonnet on, wear your Sunday's best because you never know who you'll meet. Eat healthy, don't wear tight shoes, keep your hair done, nails and toes done, sit up straight, wear heels, save your money, travel, and enjoy your life. Do all you can before getting married and having children if this is what you want. Then when you do decide to have a family, keep living it up even more! Your life doesn't end where your child's life begins, not if you do it right. Remember to never compare yourself to other people's situations because what may seem like a fairytale on the outside, could just be a beautiful lie, with the ugly truth sitting underneath the surface. Be happy, be grateful, and live out *your* life of purpose!

Love Always,

Mommy

Acknowledgements

As I look over my life, I understand why things happened the way they did. I was being guided by a higher power. The twists, turns, and decisions that I perceived as wrong were stepping stones for where I am today. Everything I've been through has made me everything I am.

I remember watching a YouTube clip with Oprah and Gary Zukav and learning about the soul. That's when it hit me that even when I thought I was alone I wasn't. There was always something guiding me. All I needed to do was be still. I am now aware of the ship in my life and even when life gets cloudy, I am able to regroup and get back on course.

I am grateful for my soul. It gives me courage to keep moving forward, and I feel confident that in the midst of despair, there is purpose. There is a divine in me that sees and knows even when I don't. I can rest assure that my steps are ordered, and when I am still I give power to the manifestation.

My life is no mistake and I don't believe in coincidences. Everything I've encountered has made me stronger. The good and *bad* decisions, the mistakes, and the wrong-doings were lessons, and I've grown from them all. I've gone through some storms and I am sure there will be more, but as I type this I know that I am flourishing. For that, I am grateful.

There have been a few people who have been instrumental to my journey and I want to acknowledge their importance in my life. My dear mother Judelle Stokes. I admire you and your strength I don't know where I would be without you. Thank you for never giving up on me. You have taught me that life isn't a rehearsal and I live by that every single day.

Friends, old and new, have played a huge role in my growth. They were apart of many of those lessons that taught me to be okay with who I am. I had to learn to be secure. I learned that it is okay to be by myself when people leave unexpectedly. It was hard, but I made it. Those lonely experiences were catalysts for my growth and I am thankful. I learned to accept myself. I learned to love myself.

Daniel *Honey*, you are everything to me and I love you so much. Although things didn't work out, I want to thank you for everything you've done for me. I am so very grateful for the three children we have. I appreciate you for being an excellent father. You have taught me so much. One thing that sticks out to me the most is to love unconditionally. Throughout all that we've been through, you have always shown your love for me. I thank you for taking care of me when I was not at my best. I thank you for supporting me in all of my endeavors. You are truly an angle in my eyes. Thank you for loving me and being a wonderful father. I truly appreciate you and love you to the moon and back.

Having the twins, Trevor and Travis, has been a blessing. The lessons I've learned are invaluable. Going from no kids to two was a journey, but it has helped me develop into the woman I am today. You have laid the foundation for my story. I thank you for my vision and I truly understand that everything happens for a reason. It was really hard in the beginning. However, it has strengthened me to become a better mom. I love you guys you are my rock, my foundation and I will do anything for you. Thank you for being good children. You are the reason I feel like I can do anything. You both have encouraged me to be a better mom by finishing school. You inspired this book and I thank you. You have been so sweet to me. I love you so much and I appreciate you for letting me be your mom. I have no regrets; you boys are my true miracle and I thank you for loving me. You are so respectful and I admire the power you have at such a young age. You are going in the right direction. You will be stand up men and I am excited for your future because I know you will prosper in whatever you do. I am a proud mother of twin boys. Not everyone can have twins. Thank you, God, for this true blessing. I can't wait to do more traveling with you. You both are like little men always wanting the best out of life and to save money. You deserve the best out of life and that is what I and your father will continue to provide. I am excited about our everlasting journey together. I love you!

Ngozi Obiaku Baier, I can't believe I have a beautiful daughter. In the first year of your life, you've taught me patience. It's hard having a little one running around, but you have really lit a fire under me that I cannot put out. You are the reason for me completing my book. After finding out I was pregnant I didn't know what to do. It was hard. However, I soon learned that you were the answer to it all. You changed my life, Gogo. You help me to be diligent in all that I do. You taught me to find my true happiness. So that's what I did. I feel fortunate to be your mother. Your name means blessings, and that's what you've been to my life. You don't understand now, but one day we will talk and I will explain it all. You won't have to follow in my footsteps. You will know better the first time. I love you so much, Blessings, and this book is dedicated to you.

As genuine as I want to be in my acknowledgements, I can't possibly thank every single person because I would have to write another book. However, I would like to say thank you to the grandparents Mr. and Mrs. Baier. Thank you for helping me with the children. If it weren't for you all I don't know where I would be. It has been a journey with three children so I thank you all for giving me mommy time when it was needed. I thank you for being a listening ear and I truly thank you for just supporting me during the times when I couldn't handle all that was on my plate. Thank you!

David *Precious* Johnson, you've helped me so much, I don't know if you know that or not. You are the person I hate to disappoint. I liken you to God in some ways. I can't really explain it, but I want you to know that you truly bring the best out of me. Thank you for being there. I aspire to be as grounded as you are, you are truly one of a kind.

To Ms. Sharita *Fierce* Pierce, we have known each other for years. I appreciate your growth. I see that you are blossoming into a beautiful woman. I remember our conversation a while back where we discussed not feeling like women even though we were both of age. You are a woman, a beautiful one and I am proud of you for reaching your goals. You have shown me that life is what you make it. You remind me of Gina Parnell. Thank you for inspiring me to be transparent. I was nervous, but I am grateful I have people like you in my corner who encourage me to face my fears

Ms. Cynthia Iya Mboe, God bless your soul. I know you are still with me because when I lose things you help me find them. I miss you so much and I just want to let you know that I do feel your presence around me. Thank you for being my angel. I just want you to know that when I met you, you gave me a sense of hope in my most depressing days. Around the time I met you I was pregnant with twins. I felt like I would never be the youthful girl I was before kids. However, you helped me reconnect to my outgoing, creative, and fun side. It seemed like every weekend you were in some country or a new state living your best life. I really admired how you embraced life as a single woman. I lived through you. I miss the times we had because it was always fun around you. You were the true Gina Parnell because you stayed put together at all times. Thank you for your beauty, classiness, and brains. I thank you for allowing me the opportunity to experience being around your beautiful friends. You were such a classy lady and that is something I will always admire about you. You've inspired me to do so much and I really miss you.

My YouTube favorites, life coaches Shanel Cooper Sykes, Leticia Padua, Angel Richardson, Baje Fletcher, Mark Haughton, and Detroit's own Courtney Sanders, you all have really been an amazing asset to my life. I don't know if a thank you is enough however, I just want to say that you have truly changed me for the better. I acknowledge you because I found you at a time in my life of uncertainty. I was absolutely at my lowest and didn't know how to get out of that sunken place. I thank you for teaching me true life lessons that I had no clue existed. I simply existed until I found your channels. It is my goal to be to someone what you all have been to me.

To all the people who helped me bring my vision to life, Laneshia Lamb, Mikhaella Norwood, King Ray Tucker, Gloria Person, Iyanna V. Stokes, Justin Alexander Gordon, Bre'ann White, Stephan J. Phillips, Tay Sands, Nakija Mills, Juaqueen Keem Gunn, Carmen D. White, Lauren Beverly, P1Design (https://www.fiverr.com/p1design), Karthik Kuntumala, Roger Tucker, Loretta Humphrey-Cruz, Adam Stokes, Knight Light Candle CO LLC, Sunni Dai thank you. I truly appreciate you from the bottom of my heart. Thank you for dealing with my Gemini ways. I know I can be difficult. Our connection is not by chance. As a team, we will do great things and I am so appreciative of your support during this project. I am excited about the future. "Don't Be That Girl: The American Dream Is Not Your Reality" will be a best seller! It will reach millions of women, helping them to be better in their walk of life. Again, thank you!

Dear Single Women

I am jealous of you! You can get up and go to work or school, then come home to go to sleep the rest of the day. When you need time to yourself, you have it. Although the same is possible for me, it's certainly not easy! I have to plan and make arrangements with people. I have to make sure the people I make arrangements with are good people. You, on the other hand, can leave without having to answer to anybody. If you want to leave and go out of town for days at a time, you can.

Single women, I am upset with some of you! You don't understand how good you have it. Some of you take your single years for granted by rushing to the next stage of life instead of living in the moment. You look at married women and wish that it were you without understanding her circumstances. You don't listen to mothers when we say it's hard.

I'll be honest with you - I don't like being a mother. It's one of the hardest jobs I have ever had. Before children, I would come and go as I pleased. I could come and go as I pleased. My entire life had always been my choice. If I didn't like something, I could change it. Today, things are a lot different.

Single women, please live your life! Understand, everything that glitters, isn't necessarily gold. Sometimes singular is better than plural. Spend time with yourself and be selfish because you have the opportunity to do so. If you're single and have yet to become a mother, you're pulling your own strings. You're able to do all the things us women on the other side, daydream about. Don't take it for granted!

CHAPTER 1

The Pill That Started It All

Writing this book has been a challenge because it has forced me to face everything about myself, even the things I don't like. There were moments when I had to stop. I felt like sugar coating my experiences because I was embarrassed. I know how judgmental people can be and I had to ask myself if I was ready to stand in that kind of spotlight.

I called my dear friend and I told her what was going on, how I was feeling. She straight up told me that it wouldn't be fair for me to write this *type* of book without sharing my whole truth. I couldn't share other people's experiences without sharing my own. So here it is.

There was a time in my life when I needed validation. My hope was that I would get it from my relationships. When I met my children's father and he shared how he'd lost his wife and child, I felt obligated to replace what he'd lost. He was in mourning and I wanted to fill his void. Almost like filling his void would fill mine.

I gave so much of myself to him, willingly. I thought that if he got what he wanted, I would too. Not realizing that everything that I was giving away was literally taking from me. I was looking for validation, but I didn't know what it looked like. I wasn't sure what it should feel like. Hell, I didn't even know what I should feel after getting it.

Time passed and I realized I had forgotten about myself. It pains me to write this, but I actually took fertility pills to get pregnant. Yes, you read that correctly. The woman who is warning you about having children, purposely had hers. And, I guess, that's why I can warn you because I've been there. I know what it feels like to have clouded vision.

I had no idea what I was getting myself into. I remember telling him that I didn't want kids. That I wanted to finish school, get engaged, travel and *eventually* get married. I had my American Dream in mind, but I became sidetracked by his needs and what was happening all around me. My friends were getting pregnant. They were raising children, and they made it look so easy.

I went to see my doctor and told him I wanted to have children. I told him that my boyfriend wanted kids but wasn't ready to get married. He warned me to not move forward with it, but I didn't listen. I was too focused on the kids my boyfriend wanted and the curiosity I had about having one of my own.

Let me tell you about love...when you have more of it for someone else than you have for yourself, you will do some crazy things. I wanted to make him happy. Kids would do that. That's what I told myself. I was so lost, unsure of myself and without any real guidance.

Things really took a turn for the worst when I moved out of the apartment that I manifested for myself. When I moved in with him, I didn't have to lift a finger. The bills were paid and I was comfortable. The worst thing that can happen to someone who's lost is for them to become comfortable in their own destruction.

I told my cousin that I was taking the pills and she told me to stop before I ended up with triplets. After hearing her say that, I got scared. I stopped taking the pills that same day. Not too long after, I started seeing signs that I needed to move on. We argued. We fought. And with the passing of each day, it became clearer that this wasn't where I needed to be.

Just when I was ready to call it quits, I found out I was pregnant. Do you know how much courage it took for me to walk away from somebody who took care of my every need? How difficult it was for me to say goodbye to the provider of my so-called *validation*? It took for him to embarrass me in front of my friends for me to say, "I've had enough," but by that time it was too late. My cousin was wrong about the pills. I didn't have triplets, I had twins.

I felt trapped. On top of the fact that my self-esteem was at an all time low, I had nowhere to go. I had to face this head-on. I didn't have a choice. This was it. The life that had so much promise, the one I had taken for granted, was now completely over...at least that's how I felt.

I am the girl that I don't want you to be, and as hard as it was for me to tell you that it was my fault too, I knew I had to for you to truly get it. Please don't do what I did. Don't be who I was. Now that I am older, I know who I am and I realize the mistakes I've made. I am finally at a place where I can separate myself from the things that are not fruitful for my life. I can now walk away without any regrets.

I love my children dearly. I love being their mom but I do not like the responsibilities of being a mother. Their father is amazing and although we did not work out, we have an awesome relationship and are able to co parent. I didn't live society's American Dream, but I feel like I had a taste of something relatively close. We had a beautiful home with our three children. I drove a nice car and he was a provider. I didn't have to work. I was well taken care of; I just wasn't happy.

For ten whole years I wasn't living up to my full potential. I actually let myself go. I was existing *don't be that girl.* Be the girl that moves to the beat of her own drum and understands that the American dream is whatever reality you wish to make it.

I am dancing now, y'all. I do what makes me happy and that freedom has made me a better mother. I am putting myself first, which means when I show up for my children, *I show up*! Ladies, don't forget about yourself. We can't be good mothers, good friends, and good people if we aren't first good to ourselves.

The flight attendant instructs you to put the mask on yourself first, in the event of an accident, before attempting to save anyone else. That rule isn't just for flying on planes, it's also for flying in life. Take care of you first. Take it from me. Live your dreams and walk in your single lifestyle proudly. Consider me your Single Woman Advocate, I've been there and I've done that. It's not some bad place like people make it seem this space is a good one, embrace it girl!

CHAPTER 2

The American Dream Is Not Your Reality

When you hear the phrase "The American Dream", what kind of thoughts does it illicit? For many, it looks like striking it big with a great career, owning a large house and driving a fancy car. For many women, it means even more; it means that in addition to this, this American Dream involves being a young wife and eventually expanding that family of two into a family of four or maybe even more! Sure, this may be a nice dream to make a reality from the outside looking in, but I have found out for myself, that it is not all it's cracked up to be.

As I look back over my life, I catch myself daydreaming of simpler days. I think back to when I was single, living in a one-bedroom apartment with my whole life ahead of me. I had no idea how much freedom I had until I no longer had it. When I woke up, my days were mine to plan. Outside of work, I chose where I spent my time and who I spent it with, and as I lived this life of no restraint, I neglected to see the blessing in it.

Isn't that so typical? We're so busy living that we forget that we're alive. We forget to breathe; not just to take in air, but to actually breathe. Our lives become so customary and routine that we get to the point where we are numb to it. As the newness of transitions fade, it all melts back into just seeming like another day. Life changes fast. If you blink you will miss that space in between then and now.

One moment I was single, and the next, I was in "a situationship" with twins! My twins are seven and my daughter isn't quite one yet, and quite frankly, I have no idea how I got here. Well obviously, we all know how I got here, but really, *how* did I get here? At what point in my life did my priorities change? When did I begin to disregard the good times of the single life and begin to subconsciously search for something new?

The truth is, I never took the time to enjoy my single days. I expected them and did not appreciate them. I was in a hurry to live life, taking for granted how good I had it. I see the same from women around me. Moving way too fast with men they barely know, giving up their identity for a life that *appears* to be more appealing, a life resembling the typical, cookie cutter version of the American Dream. It hurts me to watch. Hell, it hurts me to experience it, especially when I know that the true American Dream is the life that you intentionally make for yourself. In short, the real American Dream is whatever *you* want it to be!

I can walk down the street right now and find a woman with two or three children. I bet if I asked her to tell me how it feels to be a mom, she would tell me it's hard. Damn right it's hard! Your entire life changes. A lot of the women I know are single mothers. They were with the man long enough to make him a father, but sadly, he wasn't the one. Now that you've made it more than three pages into the book, I feel we can consider ourselves as friends, right? Good, let me share something with you: just because you have the ability to have a child, doesn't mean that you *should* have one (at least not right now)! To be honest, I don't know if you can ever be totally prepared for parenthood; however, there are situations that are a lot better off than others.

Let's be clear, I don't regret having children. They are my pride and joy, but the reality is that parenting is like night and day when compared to the single life. I had no idea what becoming a mom would be like. There were no books that spoke to my experience or even family members that I could confide in. I wish, desperately, that there was something or someone who would have shared with me just how hard it all truly was going to be.

Everybody's experience is different, and perhaps that's why there isn't a book I can personally relate to. However, my journey has connected me with other mothers that have similar sentiments. They had no warning and, to this day, have no blueprint. We are all out here just figuring things out as we go many of us making poor decisions along the way. That's why I was inspired to write this book!

I wrote this book because I care about the women around me that I see starting to head down the wrong path due to sheer lack of knowledge. I figure, if I write a book and make a movement of it, someone will have their "aha" moment. I want to shed light on what single mothers experience and even what wives experience. No matter how nice many of us make it sound, how easy it may seem, that's not the whole truth. Take this journey with me, as I put myself in the shoes of women all over the world and share their stories. Experience their ups. Bare their downs. Most of all learn from their mistakes as you learn to carve out your own intentional space in life. Envision yourself in a totally new way, living out your personal rendition of the American Dream!

Candace

CHAPTER 3

Being Mommy Is All I Know

When Candace had her daughter, it wasn't happily ever after. Instead it was, "here we go again". She wasn't married to the man of her dreams, not even close. Candace got pregnant by Jerry, a guy who has lived down the street from her all of her life. Before you ask, no, it was not one of those romantic *Love and Basketball* types of situations. He was convenient companionship and that's exactly how he treated her, even after the baby came.

Candace would call and tell me stories of how tired she was because Isabel had kept her up all night. She was teetering somewhere between being sad and mad as hell. In just under a year, her life had changed completely, and she was not prepared in the least.

Candace still stayed at home. She wanted to move out, but she couldn't afford the rent. For now, she was stuck in her mother's two-bedroom apartment. I remember the first time she went to the WIC office. She asked me to tag along. When we walked into the office, every seat was taken. We had to stand by the door. Babies were crying, children were running around, and mothers looked tired and frustrated. She and I looked at each other as it began to sink in for us both just how much life was about to change. Some women feel relief when they see others in similar situations. Not me. I was just as scared for her after seeing those women, as I was before we walked in.

It seemed like it took forever for us to be seen. When the social worker finally called us back, we walked down a short hallway into her office. Candace sat down while I stood holding Isabel. She had to fill out so many pages, and they were all in her business. I guess that's what you sign up for when you're using government assistance. I watched as Candace wrote down how much she made, which at that time wasn't much. They even asked about the child's father, who and where he was, as well as his social security number. She hesitated on those questions. I don't know what she was feeling. I didn't ask, but I am sure she didn't feel good about being in this predicament. Meanwhile, Jerry carried on with his life as if nothing had changed.

It sucks, but that's how it is sometimes. Our loneliness drives us to men who aren't good for us. Sometimes, we are so overcome by the convenience of their presence that we ignore all the red flags. The comments he made about not wanting a family when you thought he was joking, was actually him showing himself. The fact that he only comes over in the middle of the night and leaves before day break. You thought it was because he had to work, but it was because he had reduced you to his fun buddy. Let's not forget how he never wants to date you and take you out. You all don't leave the house and you don't see each other outside of those "fun" hours. If that's what you're looking for - more power to you; but if you know you want more, pay attention to the red flags so you don't end up left behind like Candace. Men have the ability to make babies, but that doesn't mean they're willing or ready to be fathers.

Remember that old saying, "momma's baby, daddy's maybe"? The baby exits us as women, so there is no doubt who the mother is. With men, well, it's an entirely different story. Only the seed exits them, giving them just cause to question who else's seed may be entering us! They don't carry the child for nine months, they aren't building that bond with the child growing inside them. This is even more reason for us to pay special attention to how and with whom we choose to give ourselves. A few moments of fun aren't worth a lifetime of struggle, heartache, and pain.

Candace learned the hard way. Actually, I question whether she ever really learned at all. When she and Jerry decided to become intimate, her life changed immediately. Within a year, she was having a baby and he was avoiding her calls. Yet, Candace didn't stop putting herself in those predicaments. Within five years of Isabel, she had Jacob, Derrick, and Marie, all of whom have different fathers.

We stopped having baby showers after Jacob. It became clear that Candace was spiraling out of control. Before you give me the side eye, allow me to explain. Candace still worked at the same job she had when Isabel was born. The one where she wasn't making enough to take care of just the two of them. She continued to deal with guys exactly like Jerry. They never called and if they did stop by, it was never for long. Candace's poor mom was getting tired of her way of living so she finally told Candace that she needed to move out and start standing on her own two feet. Unfortunately, Candace had no clue what that was like.

When she began to look for housing, she found that her only options were the projects on the other side of town. She submitted her application, releasing even more personal information. They approved her, and she was finally on her own. For most people, this would be a time of celebration but Candace couldn't celebrate. She was too busy being scared. This would be the first time that she would be alone with all of her children. She was terrified, but she played it cool in front of all of us. We all helped her move. She asked us to stay over like old times but none of us were interested in a sleepover including four children, all under the age of six. I stayed a little longer than everyone else, simply because I wanted to check on her. I could see the fear all over her face.

Crazy thing is, Candace was so smart. She could have been anything she wanted. She can *still* be anything she wants, but she has given up on herself. Candace is content with the benefits she receives. She is content with the apartment they've given her. *The guys never spend the night anyway*. She joked about the strict rules the housing authority had for its tenants. Candace figured this was a good set up. She could tell the guys to leave before they had the chance to tell her they were leaving.

Candace wore a smile as she pushed a double stroller she snagged from goodwill. Isabel walked at her side and Derrick was wrapped against her chest. I asked her how it felt to be a mother. She looked away to reflect, as if this question was loaded and so must be the answer. After a few moments, she turned to me and said, "Being a mother is a constant struggle, but it's all I know."

Sheila

CHAPTER 4

Raymond Was Really Ray-Ray...

It was Friday and that only meant one thing: girl's night out! Sheila and her friends had a standing date. Every week they would pile into one of their cars and head to a nightspot. Most times they would start at the bar and make their way to the club. This Friday started the same as all the rest, but it surely ended differently.

They arrived at the club a little after eleven. As soon as they walked in, they were approached by a group of guys. Before the night was over, they were all paired off either tucked away in some corner of the dark club or sweating it out on the dance floor. Sheila and Raymond were seated having drinks. They spent the night screaming over the loud music in an attempt to get to know one another. Raymond was nice looking. He was tall, dark, and handsome, exactly what Sheila was into. And, he had a good job. He was a manager over at the Chrysler plant. Sheila felt like she had hit gold. She pouted a little when the lights came on, silently hoping Raymond would ask for her number. He did.

For the next few days, they talked non-stop. They discussed work, family, and their goals. And for the first time in over two years, Sheila missed girl's night out to hang out with Raymond. She was expecting bells and whistles for their first date, based on their conversation. He said that he would pick her up at eight, so she waited downstairs. When he drove up, she was surprised. One of his friends from last Friday was driving and Raymond was on the passenger side. He hopped out of the car and his homeboy drove off, but not before he hollered, "Get your girl to drop you off Ray Ray!"

Sheila was in a state of shock as she watched the man she had been day dreaming about for the last week get dropped off for their date. Well, at least he was dressed nicely. Raymond walked up to Sheila and pulled her in close and whispered, "Hey baby", in her ear. He smelled good. A little of Sheila's excitement returned.

"Hey Raymond! I didn't realize you didn't have a car." Sheila spoke up.

"I do, it's just in the shop right now. Do you mind driving? Sorry I didn't mention it earlier. I didn't think it would be a big deal." He responded smoothly.

Sheila paused a few seconds before reaching into her purse for her keys. They headed towards her car, which wasn't much but it was hers. She was caught off guard by all of this and wasn't sure how to respond quite yet. They continued the ride in silence to the restaurant.

When they arrived, Raymond jumped out of the car and opened the door for her. He grabbed her hand softly as he helped her out of the car. Sheila began to feel a little less tense. He was a sweet guy. He probably just had car trouble, everything would be alright.

Dinner went well. The check arrived, Raymond paid and they left. By the time they made it back to her side of the town, she realized she needed to drop him off somewhere. So, she asked him the address. He told her he wasn't ready to leave her yet, then suggested they have a nightcap. Sheila wasn't too enthused about the idea of him coming to her place yet since they had just met. Before she could contest the idea, he spoke up. Raymond shared that he really liked her and he didn't realize just how much until that very moment. He then said it would be better if they took their time.

He gave Sheila the address and she drove him to meet his homeboy. She wondered why he wasn't going home but didn't really think much of it. She dropped him off and headed back to her place. It felt different being at home on a Friday night when she was so used to hanging with her girls. She called her friend Jessica who told her they all were still out. Sheila wasn't quite ready to go home yet, so she made a U-turn and met up with them instead. Surprisingly, they were just down the block from where she had dropped Raymond off.

Her friends were excited to see her and wanted to hear details from the night. Sheila told them how sweet he was, and they all smiled in excitement for her. For them, that was cause enough to celebrate. Jessica ordered double shots for everybody. The music was loud, the lights were low, and the bartender kept the drinks coming. Within an hour, Sheila was twisted out of her mind. Jessica tapped her on the shoulder and told her that Raymond had just walked in. Excited, Sheila jumped up from their VIP table and ran into his arms. The remainder of the night, she and Raymond were wrapped up in each other's embrace. By the time the lights came on, Sheila was sloppy drunk and not ready for the party to end.

On the sidelines, Jessica watched and smiled. This was the first time that Sheila had ever let her guard down this much. "It's about time she let loose like us", Jessica thought to herself. Raymond carried Sheila to her car, then walked around to the driver's side. He hadn't drunk much at all, so he was good to drive. On the drive home, Sheila mumbled about not wanting to be alone. Raymond reassured her that he had her and she smiled just before passing out on his shoulder.

The next morning all Sheila remembered was their date. Her head was throbbing and she had apparently slept on the couch. Her clothes were strewn all over the floor and Raymond was on the opposite end of the couch. This was not the first date she had planned. She quickly jumped up and grabbed her clothes. Her living room reeked of alcohol. This was not good. She couldn't even remember if she had used protection.

After she showered and got dressed, she went downstairs to find that Raymond had left. No note, no text, no nothing. He was gone. She searched the room for her phone. It was lodged between the seat cushions. Sheila scrolled through her call log to find his number. The phone rang, but no answer. She dialed again. Same result. She checked her home to make sure nothing was stolen, then dialed up Jessica.

She answered just before her voicemail picked up. She sounded like she was still asleep. Sheila pleaded for her to get up. She explained what had happened and asked Jessica to call Ray's friend, Shawn to see if this was some kind of sick joke. By this time, Jessica was wide awake. Fortunately for Sheila, Shawn was lying next to Jessica. She put the phone down to confer with him. Five-minutes-later she picked up the phone and told Sheila that Raymond was really Ray-Ray. He worked at Chrysler, but he wasn't the manager. He was actually an hourly employee. As a matter of fact, he had just started. And, Ray-Ray didn't have a car, at all. Sheila listened in horror as it sunk in that she didn't know this guy at all. Not only had she given him her time and undivided attention, she had given him herself. Sheila started to hyperventilate. On the other end of the phone, Jessica yelled, "I'm on my way."

By the time she arrived, Sheila was curled up in a ball. Jessica pleaded with her to get it together. She tried everything she could to lift her spirits but nothing worked. All Sheila could think about was if she had a disease? Jessica informed her that she needed to schedule an appointment to get checked. She called her physician and was able to explain what had happened. The physician informed her that she needed to wait a few weeks to be tested. Sheila set up an appointment two-weeks from that date and began the agonizing wait.

The next two-weeks were hell as she anxiously waited for her appointment. Raymond attempted to call and explain himself a few times, but Sheila didn't answer. She did, however, listen to his voicemails. He sounded sincere in his apologies but she wasn't about to entertain him. At least not until she got those test results.

When the day finally came for her appointment, everything seemed to happen so fast. They called her back, she was tested, and then it was time to go. Sheila left the doctor's office on a high. She had never been so happy and relieved in her life. There were no signs or symptoms of disease. She had him test her for everything under the sun, and all of her results were negative. He made another appointment for her in six weeks as a standard follow up and sent her on her way. As soon as she made it to her car, she called Jessica. She told her that her results were negative and that she had to come back in a few weeks as part of standard procedure. Jessica asked her had she talked to Raymond. Apparently, he had been asking everybody about Sheila. Everyone in the neighborhood knew that he was sorry.

Sheila hadn't talked to Raymond. She preferred to keep her distance, but that didn't keep him from calling. He had called every single day since the morning he disappeared. Jessica told Sheila to talk to Raymond and give him a chance to explain. She said he seemed to be a good guy; he just had a lot going on. Sheila wasn't sure she wanted to be in the midst of anything he had going on. As much as she told herself not to, Sheila ended up answering Raymond's call. He told her how much he missed her and that he was sorry. Sheila remained quiet. He explained that he left without a word because he had to go to work. He was late, and already had two strikes. Raymond told Sheila that although he did work at the Chrysler plant, he wasn't a supervisor. Instead, he was an hourly employee that was on probation. Sheila just listened as he confirmed everything that his homeboy had already told her and Jessica. He wasn't doing a good job of making Sheila feel better about allowing him back into her life but at least he was honest. He went on to share that he was having trouble keeping jobs. Raymond had a rough life and every time it seemed he was getting things together, things fell apart even more.

He shared intimate details about his mother, how she babied him and wouldn't let him spread his wings. His father wasn't in his life. He had several children strung all over town and he didn't provide for any of them. Raymond's mother wasn't shy about reminding him that he would end up just like his dad, and apparently that messages sunk in. Sheila felt sorry for him. Raymond continued for what seemed like hours, telling her about his job, his family, his goals, and how much he wanted her in his life. Sheila wasn't prepared for that last part but her recent doctor's test results made her a little more open to the idea, especially now that she had heard the whole truth directly from him.

Raymond asked her out again. Sheila asked him would she have to drive, but she already knew the answer. She said she'd call him back after she cooked dinner, but she had already cooked. She really just wanted to call Jessica to give her the rundown. When Jessica answered the phone, Sheila wasted no time telling her everything that had just happened. Jessica cheered Raymond on but Sheila still wasn't impressed. Jessica told her to calm down and remember that everyone makes mistakes. Jessica encouraged Sheila to give Raymond another chance, likely because Jessica and Raymond's friend were spending a lot of time together. They were dancing pretty close to being in a relationship. No wonder Jessica was in support of their union .An hour later, Sheila and Raymond were back on the phone. They made plans to go out on their second date that following weekend.

The next few weeks flew by, and Sheila was caught up in a whirlwind of emotions. She was excited to have companionship and happy that Raymond was nice, but the events of their first date continued to replay in her mind. She mentioned it to Jessica who told her she was tripping, so Sheila tried to relax. Things were going pretty well. Raymond was at her house every other night. Sheila made sure to wake him up for work when he stayed. Before she knew it, it was time for her follow up appointment.

When she got to her doctor's office, she felt different. Sheila had a bad feeling. The nurse called her back. Sheila followed her into the bathroom. She gave her the rundown on the urinalysis and then walked out. Sheila did as she was told then walked back to the waiting area. About twenty minutes later, the doctor called her back. The look on his face let her know that something wasn't right. Her heart sank into the pit of her stomach as she stood to join him in the hallway.

The doctor asked her how she had been feeling the last few weeks. Sheila hadn't really thought about it until now, but she had been feeling a little different. She was experiencing headaches and the smell of certain food made her nauseous. "I hate to tell you this, but you're pregnant." Sheila's legs grew weak. She almost collapsed. Luckily, the nurse was standing near the door and caught her. The nurse asked if Sheila was okay. She wasn't. She and Raymond hadn't even had sex since the first night and they certainly were nowhere near ready to be parents.

For the rest of the day, Sheila was a zombie. Usually, she would call Jessica, but she wasn't sure she could talk to anybody about this, so she ended up not calling anyone at all. Not Jessica, not Raymond...no one! In her need to wrap her head around the fact that she would be a mother, all Sheila could do was go home, crawl into the bed, and cry.

The next day, Sheila woke to Raymond beating on the door. She pulled herself out of bed. She walked past the mirror and saw the remnants of yesterday's news plastered all over face. Her eyes were swollen. Tears that had since dried up, stained the sides of her face. She headed toward the door, where she could hear Raymond huffing and puffing about missed calls. She opened the door then walked toward the couch. Raymond followed closely behind her, immediately deflated at the look of Sheila. When he asked Sheila what was going on, it took her a moment to respond, "I'm pregnant."

"By who?"

Sheila looked back on that day often. After Raymond questioned her, she told him to get out. She contemplated an abortion, but she couldn't bring herself to do it. She went as far as making the appointment and sitting on the bed to have the procedure done, but she just couldn't do it. She often wondered what life would be like had she never met Raymond.

How differently would things be if she had never gone to meet her friends after their date? That night changed her life forever. It didn't matter how careful she had been up to that point. That one night changed it all.

It's amazing how one decision can change the trajectory of your life. Just one. Sheila's story isn't uncommon. I've met a few women over the years who are in Sheila's shoes. They met someone who talked a good game, but when things got rough they split. Yet another reason why we, as women, must be careful. Words don't mean half as much as actions. Sheila found that out more and more each day.

Sheila continued to work up until the day she had her son. Raymond called a few times leaving messages like, "You know I'm not ready for this." Sheila thought about the fact that she was not "ready" either, yet was still stepping up to the plate to handle her responsibilities, and she immediately became angry. He looked at her like it was her fault, as if she was the only person who played a role in this situation. She didn't make the baby by herself, so she shouldn't be left to raise him by herself either.

Even after Sheila told her how upset she was, Jessica was still excited. She continued to smile when Sheila told her that Raymond had deserted her. She even laughed heartily when Sheila told her how scared she was. Jessica couldn't see past the fact that someone would be joining her in motherhood. The fact that she would no longer be the only girl in the group who had to find a sitter, meant that Jessica would now have someone she could talk to about the highs and lows of being a mom. Secretly, this was the exact outcome Jessica had been silently hoping for. It didn't take Sheila long to figure out that Jessica wasn't her friend. Before little Bishop was born, Sheila had distanced herself from everybody. It was times like these that she wished that she and her mom were on good terms. She needed someone to talk to, someone to assure her that everything would be alright.

Unfortunately, she had to rely on herself and the things she had learned over the years. Which in actuality, wasn't much to prepare her for motherhood. Having Bishop in her life was like being on a new job without first receiving the proper training. She was learning as she went. She tried her best, and it was a lot. The fact that she had to do it all alone only compounded her problem.

After a few years, you'd think things would get easier. Not for Sheila. Although Raymond did pop up occasionally to drop off a hundred dollars here and there, he became even more distant when he realized Bishop was on the spectrum. At about four years old, Sheila had him tested at the advice of her childcare provider. His speech was delayed, he frequently had tantrums, he couldn't stand loud noises, and he had meltdowns... loud, earth shattering meltdowns.

Bishop was placed in therapy and Sheila was coached on how to handle him. Raymond disappeared and Sheila became overwhelmed. Every time she went to the store, it turned into a huge ordeal. Bishop would end up screaming and crying. Sheila would become embarrassed and end up melting down herself once she reached the car. It got to the point where she didn't want to shop for groceries while Bishop was with her, so she'd only go while on her lunch break at work, just so she could go alone. She began to medicate Bishop, putting him to sleep so she wouldn't have to hear the crying.

I knew Sheila, but we weren't best friends. I met her a few times and attempted to offer my support. She would seem open to it until it was actually time to meet up, then she would make an excuse. I heard from one of our mutual friends that she was embarrassed. That hurt me a little, that she thought I would judge her or her son. We spoke on the phone a few times, and as soon as it would seem like he was getting ready to turn up, she would give him a pill. Within thirty-minutes, the background would be quiet. I mentioned to her that maybe she should find an alternative to giving him sleeping pills. She got upset with me and we haven't talked since.

I feel for Sheila and other women like her. Women who are in over their heads before they even get a chance to enjoy life. Women who are overwhelmed and have no one to turn to. Women who want solutions, but don't know where to find them or how to use them once they do. It's a lot, being a mother, then add in our insecurities and issues that were there before the baby and, well, you just get a colossal mess. How does one heal themselves while raising a child? At some point, you would think that our healing has to be placed on the backburner so that our children have all of our focus, but in that case, are we really beneficial to our families when we are still broken ourselves? It seems, the greatest gifts require some of the biggest sacrifices.

Victoria

CHAPTER 5

I Hate To Say It, But I Told You SO

I loved Victoria. She was beautiful, quirky, and upbeat. You couldn't be around her without smiling. She was the kind of person who found the good in everything, and she made you want to do the same. I think I envied her: her life, her freedom...basically everything she had that I didn't, and all the things that I once took for granted.

However, Victoria had a different story, and because of her story, we had completely different perspectives. See, Victoria grew up with her aunt Vivian, who we all called Ms. Viv. Her aunt took her in when she was five. Her mother died and her dad was an alcoholic. Ms. Viv took really good care of her, but that didn't stop Victoria from daydreaming about her own family. She wanted *her* mother and *her* father, but that was a luxury she would never possess. She was a child stripped from her foundation at a very young age, so it made sense that she would want a family to call her own. My fiancé and I represented everything she wanted.

My fiancé was an all-around great guy who saw to it that our boys and I were well taken care of. Victoria saw what we represented, a mom and dad under the same roof with their children, and she envied us for it. No matter how much I told her to embrace where *she* was in life, it only stood to make her more jealous. Every time I gave her the wise advice to simply appreciate her own journey, it only fell on deaf ears. She looked past my struggles and saw only the *picture* she painted in her mind. Victoria saw the family she always wanted, and with that, it was only a matter of time before my struggles became hers.

I remember so vividly the in-depth conversations she and I had about my depression, and how deeply I had sunken into it. I asked myself repeatedly, how did I get here? One time, I posted on Facebook, "What have I done?", and I received countless responses of confusion. People did not understand where I was coming from. When I made that post on Facebook, it was to vent without venting, however, receiving the feedback that I did, only confused me more. Those comments made me feel like a horrible person because I was second-guessing my decision to have children at that stage in life. As I look back on it, I honestly feel that women are happy when new mothers are born because they have one more person to experience it all with. They are now in the same position with the same limitations. They both now live within the same confines.

I don't want to downplay motherhood or dress it up as this dreaded thing. It's a beautiful thing, provided that your life is ready for it and you are mentally prepared for the shift that will take place. In those cases, having a baby is wonderful and expected! However, when you're immature and a poor decision maker who is unsure of what to do from one day to the next, I'm sorry but a baby is NOT the best thing for you.

I shared all of this with Victoria. I let her know exactly how I felt. I let her know how much I cried and how overwhelmed I was. I shouldn't have expected her to really understand it because at that point, she wasn't open minded. She wasn't open to the full picture. Victoria was only open to the part that she needed. Everything else, she was willing to deal with when the time came. When our wants are so strong, they overpower our ability to listen. That's another reason I decided to write this book. It gives you the opportunity to read both sides of the story with the good and the bad. This way, you don't have the ability to see me, and be persuaded by the *picture* that appeals to you the most.

I share all of this with you because nothing has been more devastating to me than to see my friend's spirit broken as she took on burdens she wasn't prepared for. Victoria wanted my situation so badly, she was willing to do whatever she had to do to get it. Unfortunately, that meant getting pregnant by someone who was not good for her. He was simply a placeholder, *symbolizing* a father figure.

My struggles became her struggles and then some. She created what she thought she wanted without really thinking it through. When I found out she was having a baby, truth be told, I was devastated. I wanted her to enjoy her life and not rush into parenthood, because once you start, there's no going back. There is no restart, no backspace, no control, alt, and delete to this parenting lifestyle. When the baby is here, it's here, and now that she was a mother, I could see the shift. The upbeat chick that I once knew, who I loved so much because of her personality and infectious laugh, was now emitting a much dimmer light. It seemed like even though her words were still upbeat, her body language and facial expressions told a different story. She always looked beat down and overwhelmed. She looked like I did.

She's always been really strong. When you lose a parent at a young age, you have to be because there is so much that you have to deal with.

Victoria put up a fight by making me think that things were going really well for her and that there were no problems at all. She kept that charade going for a long time but I saw through it. As a parent, I could spot the overwhelmed look in her eyes, I just didn't say anything. I allowed her to bring those walls down in her own time. Eventually, she did open up and finally began to share her truth.

I still remember the conversation we had. I had been calling her, but she wouldn't answer. Then one day, I heard her voice on the other end. I could tell it was taking everything in her to sound content. Finally, I said, "Victoria, you can stop now. I know you're unhappy. I could see it all over your face the other week and now I hear it in your voice." As soon as she began talking again, the tears flowed. I sat silently on the phone, giving her time and space to release it all. By the time she got herself together, fifteen minutes had passed. She apologized but I told her it was okay, and in fact, it was actually necessary. I wasn't there to judge her. I just wanted to be her friend. I guess hearing those words shook something within her because she began to cry harder and louder.

She told me everything. Victoria gave me the rundown on how she and the guy met but he fooled her. They moved in together and he stopped working. Through our conversation, she was able to "let it all hang out" so to speak, and I could tell she was relieved. She confessed that she feared I would say, "I told you so", but I never did and never will. I'll admit that I thought it several times. I didn't want this life for her. I told her not to do it, but she didn't listen. Now here we are. Even still, I will never belittle her by saying that. Life is hard enough without the pressure of someone's judgment on our shoulders.

In the end, we have to make sure we are making good choices, and unfortunately, Victoria hadn't. Initially, all was well, but with her shift came his. He stopped being supportive and his family wasn't there for her or their child. Now, she was in a completely new space in her life and basically, she was alone. She had permanently attached herself to someone who didn't have the same passion for family that she did. Her household was unequally yoked.

As if a new baby wasn't stressful enough, she had to also deal with an unbalanced "situationship". That's a lot for a new mother or any mother for that matter. Victoria neglected to see this until she was already in it. She was so focused on family, not realizing that family itself is simply a word. It's the people in it that provide the substance. Children don't choose their families, but as women, we choose who we build those families with. In a split second of poor decision making, we can connect ourselves to someone who can bring us more heartbreak than heart warmth. I wish Victoria had considered this. We have to really be smart in who we choose to give ourselves to. Otherwise, we are setting ourselves up for a continuous uphill battle.

This was Victoria's story. She saw something she wanted and didn't stop until she had it. Sure, Victoria had a beautiful baby who she loved and who loved her back, but her family was still incomplete, and her void remained. When someone speaks to you in vulnerability, take heed. It's not because they want to sour your perspective on life, or they don't want you to be happy. On the contrary, they want you to have it in the best way possible! I've learned that sometimes it's hard to see the forest while standing in it. Victoria's story symbolizes that in addition to worrying about the threat of postpartum depression and being responsible for an entire human being, we also have to deal with our co-parent. We have to make sure that when we are making these permanent decisions- *because a child is permanent-* that we do so with the future, our children, and ourselves in mind.

Alexandria

CHAPTER 6

Church Boy

Alexandria met Church Boy over the phone. At the time, she was in school and working full-time, and had just gotten out of a messy relationship. Actually, it wasn't a relationship as much as it was a situation.

Church Boy was a weird and unexpected distraction. Every time Alexandria was home, he would call the house by accident. One day in particular, the phone rang and the guy on the other end asked for Charles. The name sounded familiar. Alexandria asked the caller to describe Charles, and oddly enough, it was a guy she used to sing for. They both laughed. What a coincidence that he called for someone she actually knew. Alexandria couldn't remember if Charles had a similar number or not. Maybe it was destiny that she and Church Boy's paths crossed.

That day, their conversation was short-lived. Alexandria had to work, and she still needed to prepare for school later. Her days were jammed packed. By the time she got home, she was exhausted. She was prepared to crash when she walked into the house, only to be met with, "That boy has been calling here," from her mother. She was caught off guard but called him back anyway. A few minutes into the conversation, Church Boy asked if he could see her. Alexandria has always been reserved, she would never meet someone she didn't know, but somehow, he convinced her.

He kept talking about God, and how deeply he was into the church. She had never met a church boy before. Alexandria didn't grow up in the church, despite her family being believers. During the time when they met, she was attending a small church with one of our mutual friends. The church was nice enough, although the pastor was a little weird and he used to mention her name in his sermons. Alexandria felt welcomed though. She finally belonged. I think that's what sparked her interest in meeting Church Boy in the first place.

She met him in front of the church, ironically enough. When he arrived, her heart dropped. He wasn't her type at all. He was on the heavier side and he had a white ring around his mouth. Alexandria was polite. She introduced herself, while silently plotting how to cut the meeting short. They chatted long enough to get a good look at one another, then said their goodbyes. When Alexandria got back into her car, she made up her mind that she wouldn't see him again. Church Boy had other plans.

He was persistent and he called often. At first, she ignored him, but one day he called and she answered. He got straight to the point: "Let me take you out to dinner." Alexandria wasn't into him, but she was into eating, so she agreed. She didn't know what to expect. She was pleasantly surprised when he arrived to pick her up. He had put forth a lot more effort than the first-time-around. He looked nicer. His haircut was fresh. He wore a button-up shirt, nice jeans, and a pair of dress shoes that would make any woman look twice. Alexandria was impressed.

They ate at her favorite restaurant, Mongolian Barbeque. He looked good that night, but the food looked and tasted even better. She was glad she said yes. They ate and talked for a while and he was charming. Yes, Church Boy was full of surprises that night...one of which being the fact that he was divorced. He went on to say that he had a two-yearold daughter during the marriage. Alexandria had never dated a man with children before. The thought alone was kind of scary, but he was so smooth, she quickly forgot her fears.

After that night, they began to spend more time together. One day, Alexandria was driving while Church Boy was sitting on the passenger side. The blue lights flashed in her rearview mirror and Church Boy freaked out. He told her to say his name was Jimmy. She was confused but she obliged. After the cop drove off, he told Alexandria his driver's license was suspended. Another surprise, considering he was always driving. Despite it being an obvious red flag, they continued to date.

She eventually met his daughter and the rest of his family. Alexandria used to tell me stories about how fussy the daughter was. They ended up growing very fond of each other though. She was even close with his family. Alexandria felt like she belonged, something she'd been longing for, for years.

I don't know how the relationship began. According to her, it just happened. They used to spend nights at his house. They had fun together. Church Boy's personality captivated her and kept her drawn in. Before long, she had fallen for him. The more time they spent together, the closer they got. Which lead to sex. Alexandria enjoyed sex with him. He was the only man who made her climax. The downside though was that they had to repent afterwards. He would always blame her as if it was her fault that they had sex when in reality, he initiated all of their sexual encounters.

He was a full of surprises. One day, he called and asked her to come over to his mother's house. He took her into the basement and sat her on his lap. He pulled up his sleeve and asked her to look at his tattoo. It was in Chinese. She asked him what it meant. "Trust in God,' he told her. Alexandria felt awkward, unsure of why he was telling her this now. Church Boy began to plead for her not to get mad. At this point, Alexandria had gone from feeling awkward to outright confusion. She wondered what new surprise lay ahead. He told her the tattoo was to cover-up his ex-wife's name. Alexandria was still lost. He went on to say that he was still married. His words were a blow to the gut. The air escaped her body as she attempted to process it all. They had been dating for a while, and at no point had it seemed like he was married. Alexandria was in a state of shock. She was angry, but when she looked up at him, all she saw was sadness in his eyes. He got her. He told her he was still married, yet she let it go.

She later found out that they were, in fact, separated. She met the ex-wife. She said their marriage was over and had been over. The situation was weird. Alexandria wondered if she should leave, or if she should believe them both and let it go. She had never been in a relationship like this. The more she thought about it, the more she felt like she couldn't leave.

Church Boy used to tell Alexandria stories involving his ex-wife and how she used to cheat on him. That was the reason they were separated. While he was out working, his wife would be at the house sleeping with his friend. Alexandria became enraged listening to the stories, but she never asked what he did wrong in the relationship. She would never do that. How could his ex-wife do that to him? He was so sweet! Alexandria was in love, and every time she looked Church Boy in his eyes, she fell deeper under his spell.

About a year or so into their relationship, Alexandria and Church Boy moved in together. Things were moving fast, but she was happy. One weekend, they decided to take a road trip to Atlanta together. When his family and friends saw Alexandria, the first question they asked was "Are you pregnant?" They both were shocked. Alexandria hadn't even considered that. She had been feeling sick for a while, but pregnancy was not on her radar. Things had been moving fast, but neither of them were ready for this. Alexandria was still young, and she didn't know anything about being a mother. Sure, she had his daughter at the house a lot of the time but that was different.

As luck would have it, or maybe it was God, Alexandria was pregnant, and yet in another strange turn of events, she had a miscarriage. Alexandria didn't cry and neither did Church Boy. She was grateful that she didn't have to worry about being a mother yet. She redirected her focus from healing her body, back to their relationship, so Alexandria started going to church with Church Boy and his family. She looked at this transition as another seal to their fate together. She belonged there with him and his family. In the beginning, things were okay. It was different than her old church, but she was with him and that's what mattered.

Things quickly changed though. The members started showing themselves, and they were mean. Alexandria would leave church feeling low. I remember talking to her for hours about how badly they made her feel, yet somehow before the end of the conversation, she would find a way to minimize their behavior.

As if that wasn't enough to deal with, Church Boy's behavior started to change. It started the day he was thrown in jail for driving without license. When Alexandria showed up to bail him out, he looked bad. He looked like he had been in there for months instead of a few hours. He walked out of the precinct and didn't even greet her. Instead, he grunted and told her to come on. Like a fool, she ran back to the car to unlock the door for him. The entire drive home, he berated her. He fussed because she had let him stay in there for so long. She didn't understand why he was being so mean when she had just used her money to get him out of jail for doing something he knew was wrong. When she tried to speak up about it, he hushed her saying that she made the choice to come and get him. She felt disrespected and undoubtedly, she was hurt.

Over the next couple of days, things were weird around the house. She didn't know what to say and neither did he apparently. He told her that he would start traveling to play music in different churches the next week. It caught Alexandria off guard because this was the first time she had heard of any of this. She assumed that it wouldn't be too bad though, considering it was for church, but she was wrong. It was bad. When he traveled, he didn't return until late at night. One night, he was so late that Alexandria grabbed his daughter and went to look for him. She called him repeatedly, but he didn't answer. She literally stayed out until 2 a.m. looking for him.

When he would finally get home, three hours later, he would act like nothing was wrong. He would say that he was at his producer's house, recording. Alexandria would let it go, even though she knew he wasn't there. Church Boy had taken her to the producer's house once and she remembered exactly where he lived. Unfortunately, she was a fool for him. Alexandria always believed whatever Church Boy told her, whether it made sense or not.

It took her a while to figure out that Church Boy was a master manipulator. He would randomly tell her that they were going to get married. Amid all of his late ramblings and lies, he actually had her convinced that they were going to live happily ever after, and she believed him. I warned Alexandria about him, but once he planted that marriage seed in her mind, she couldn't hear anything I was saying. She continued to ignore red flag after red flag while he continued to come home late and lie about it. I hoped that she would wise up, but instead she fell deeper into the abyss. After being stepped on repeatedly, Alexandria remained hopeful that Church Boy would change, but he didn't. Instead, he showed more of himself.

One evening, the producer asked them both to dinner. Alexandria happily agreed, after all, she loved food. They both got dressed and headed to her car. During their drive, Alexandria plotted on all the things she would eat while Church Boy sat quietly, preoccupied with something happening on his phone. When they arrived, the waiter showed them the table where the producer sat waiting. Things were going fine and everyone was seated and chatting, when out of nowhere the producer said, "Church Boy isn't the one for you. He needs someone better." Church Boy sat there looking weak. Actually, he didn't just sit there, he put his head down. When Alexandria finally pulled herself from her state of shock, she told the producer to mind his business, but that didn't stop him. The producer continued to berate her. Alexandria rushed to the car. Moments later, Church Boy joined her in the car. She asked him why he hadn't spoken up for her, but he didn't say a word. The remainder of the ride was silent.

Red flags were appearing all around Alexandria, more obvious now than ever. And the stink between she and Church Boy seemed to be spreading to their home. Alexandria didn't want to go back to the apartment that night because of the smell. It drove her crazy, just like he now did. At least she had the courage to ditch the house. They put in their notice and were moved within the month. The new place signified a new start for them, and for a second, it seemed like they had left the curse at the old apartment. They were both happy for a change. The incident at the restaurant began to fade into the background.

It didn't last long though. Church Boy started coming home late again. After all their time together and all he'd put Alexandria through, she had never checked his phone, but one night he came home late and she decided that she'd had enough. She grabbed his phone to see what he had been up to, and she found exactly what she was looking for. Yet, she didn't address it. She kept it to herself and remained foolishly in love.

A few months later, Church Boy told her he was moving out. Alexandria was infuriated, she wanted to fight him. She was heartbroken, and hell bent on trying to make it work, but Church Boy left anyway. Church Boy's car was in Alexandria's name. When she saw him pack his bags and head to the door, she felt compelled to do something. She told him he couldn't leave. She even contemplated reporting the car stolen. Her threats didn't work and neither did her pleas. He left and she spent the next several weeks calling him, begging him to speak with her. He ignored her, sending her into an emotional spiral. Alexandria was hurt, and she didn't know what to do. After all these years, she was single again.

Alexandria continued to go to his family's church, hoping that it would bring them back together. It didn't. His family and the rest of the congregation turned up the pressure on how they treated her. They didn't hesitate to tell her that he had gotten married the weekend after Alexandria's birthday. Her emotional low took a nosedive.

Alexandria was still in a low place, and that was nearly two years ago. Her heart was broken, and it was hard for her to pull it together. I tried to explain to her that it was for the best. Had Church Boy not left, chances are that Alexandria wouldn't have left either. Many of us as women enter relationships inexperienced, and as a result, we become paralyzed. We end up looking past red flags, unclear of what's right and wrong. If we were never shown, we have no way of knowing. Alexandria wanted to belong, and for a short period, she did. Unfortunately, she didn't receive the love that she gave.

She held onto the memories of all the good times, not realizing that those times had come to an end long ago. She stayed, hoping for better but it never came. Alexandria wanted better while settling for worse every single day. I'd never wish pain on my friend, but I'll admit that I was happy he was gone. Her healing took time, but at least she was moving in the right direction.

Over time, Alexandria became stronger. She realized that she dodged a bullet by no longer being connected to Church Boy. She joined a gym, found a new church family, and really began to work on herself. Meanwhile, Church Boy had been married three times and had two additional kids. Alexandria was almost one of those baby mothers. Ironically enough, Church Boy reached out to her to apologize. His words fell on deaf ears. Alexandria was living her best life, traveling the world, pursuing her dreams, and most of all protecting her energy from negative people.

Mona

CHAPTER 7

The Cookie-Cutter Lifestyle

Mona was the smart kid growing up. School was never a problem for her. While her friends were struggling to finish assignments and read books, she was moving on to the next project. She didn't know where she got it from, especially since her mom was a drug addict and her dad... well, she didn't know much about him. Somehow, despite all that Mona had going on around her, she managed to have a rather positive outlook on life. The way she figured it, life couldn't get worse, so she may as well enjoy the sunshine.

Growing up, Mona's grandmother played the role of her mom. Even though Mona knew she wasn't her mother, she took her in when there was nowhere else to go. She adopted Mona when her mom was unable to care for her and made sure everything was provided for. Living with her grandma provided some stability, for which, she was grateful. She vowed to herself that she would go to school and not get caught up in the life like her mom had.

High school was a breeze. Mona graduated at the top of her class and she was accepted to a list of schools all across the country. When graduation day came, Mona was floating. She was excited to be starting a new adventure even though she was a little scared at the prospect of being all alone in a new place. She smiled as she crossed the stage while her grandmother stood in the crowd clapping and yelling her name. She was so proud and who could blame her. After talking with her grandma, she decided it was time to explore the world. Luckily, Mona's grandma fully supported her, trusting in her ability to make good decisions, so when Mona told her she was moving to Texas from their home in rural North Carolina, she smiled and helped Mona plan the move.

Honestly, no one would have ever guessed that Mona would have made it. Her grandma wasn't exactly a spring chicken, so she wasn't able to help much with school. She was encouraging of course, but as for the work, Mona was on her own. Fortunately, God had big plans for her and it all came easily. Now here she was headed off to Texas studying to be a doctor. School started in late August. Mona packed only one suitcase, choosing to do all of her shopping upon arrival in her new hometown. When she landed in Texas, there was no other choice but for Mona to put her big girl panties on. She grabbed her bags from the carousel and caught a taxi to campus. Since Mona had always been a planner, she contacted the housing department before she arrived to get all of the information necessary to make her move in day flow with smooth sailing. There was a long road ahead but she was committed.

The first three years of undergrad really seemed to have flown by like birds in the wind. Mona enjoyed them but now they all seem like flickers in her past. She got as involved as she could, found a few mentors to keep her on the straight and narrow and things were going quite well. With only one year left, Mona had already passed the entrance exams for medical school and was accepted to her first-choice school. She was really doing it!

Up to that point, she had chosen not to date so the preeminence could be on her focus of finishing school and acing exams. A couple of months into Mona's senior year, she finally said yes to this guy who had been pursuing her since freshman seminar. Jeremy was nice. They both were seniors and he was preparing to go to law school. A doctor and a lawyer sounded like the perfect pairing. Their date at the spoken word cafe was nice. He even got up and performed. Mona hated to admit it, but she was impressed. He was artsy and somewhat sensitive while also being methodical, all things you have to be if your desire is to be a lawyer. They ended up spending all of their free time together falling in love.

Late November, Jeremy invited Mona to go home with him to meet his parents. She agreed provided she finished studying for a test she had on that following Monday. She spent the entire week preparing so by the time Friday came, she was ready and they took the drive to Louisiana. His parents were just as charming as he was. Over the course of that weekend, Mona was immersed in New Orleans culture and she absolutely loved it. They had great food and danced to soulful music. She was entranced by him, his family, and their roots.

By the time they arrived back in Texas, Mona made up her mind that she was ready to take their kinship to the next level. However, she decided she would wait for him to initiate the transition. Apparently, he felt the same and ended up asking her to be his girlfriend. She was happy! Despite her background, she managed to make it to Texas, outperform many of her peers, and find the man of her dreams. It all seemed too good to be true and the high continued. He gave her the space she needed to maintain her grades and she gave him the same courtesy. They understood each other. Things were going so well that she could see the finish line in the not so distant future and she knew she'd be crossing it with an awesome man.

In January, Jeremy received word that he hadn't passed the bar exam. The news tore him apart. He was no longer upbeat and sensitive. He slept more and went out less. Jeremy stop performing at the lounge, and he no longer wanted to spend time with Mona. He completely distanced himself from everything that he once held dear. Mona felt bad for him. When she attempted to be there to support him, he would push her away. At the end of the year, he still hadn't pulled himself together to successfully pass the exam while Mona was accepted into a new program. As soon as they graduated, Mona would be moving to Los Angeles and Jeremy was supposed to be coming with her, but their plans changed with little discussion.

Jeremy and Mona drifted apart, and she decided to become laser focused on school. He was her knight in shining armor, the icing on her cake, and the cherry on top. Now that he had given up on himself, she gave up on them. She attempted to revive their relationship once more before moving. He told her that he loved her, but he couldn't give her what she needed. Those words broke her heart.

Mona went off to medical school and finished at the top of her class. Jeremy reached out to her a few times. He finally passed the bar exam and eventually went to law school. A glimmer of hope danced in the pit of her stomach because she wanted him to want her back. She wanted them to hit reset on what they had. Mona wanted a lot, but apparently, he didn't. Jeremy got married...and it wasn't to Mona. When she heard the news, she buried herself deeper in her work. She offered to move her grandma out West, but she wasn't having it. She said "I was born in Carolina and I'm going to die in Carolina." Mona couldn't argue with that, even though she wanted to. She was a lot older now, and Mona couldn't get to North Carolina as much as she wanted to.

During one of Mona's visits, she asked her what happened to that nice boy from Louisiana that she was so excited about. Mona told her that he was still a nice boy, just to someone else. She told Mona that she needed to start dating again because she didn't want to leave her behind all alone. Mona would have loved to date but she rarely had the time. Besides, no one compared to Jeremy. "Why bother?" was her excuse for years, but by the time age 32 skated around, Mona was getting the itch. All of her friends from college were now married with children. Hell, their children were nearly a decade old and here she was still a virgin. She figured that she made it this long, she might as well hang on until she met the guy of her dreams and they got married. Over the next two years, Mona opened herself up to dating. She envied her friends with families. She loved her freedom but longed for companionship and voices in her house other than her own.

One of her girlfriends talked her into joining a dating website. She set up a profile and within a few hours, it seemed like everyone was in her DMs'! Most of the messages were bogus and nothing to waste time on, but there was one who caught her attention. She responded to his email and they started chatting back and forth. This continued for about a week before he asked her on a date. They met at one of the popular restaurants downtown. Shawn. He was 6'0, handsome, medium complexion and build, with a beautiful smile to top it all off.

In person, he was a lot quieter than he was online which caught her off guard. Such a difference from Jeremy, who could charm an entire room of people all at once. Mona didn't count him out though. When he did talk, it was interesting. He didn't have any children, but he wanted at least one. He was originally from California and he owned a graphic design company. They continued to date for several weeks and on Valentine's Day, he surprised her with a private chef. That night he asked

55

if she'd be interested in dating exclusively. Obviously, she said yes. Who says no to a private chef?

At this point, Mona was knocking loud and clear on 35 and she was ready to move forward in whatever direction they happened to be going in. She wanted to know what they were doing. In your thirties, it's no longer cute to casually date, at least not for Mona, a woman ready to join the ranks of those that were happily married and living the so called, American Dream. Luckily, Shawn was on the same page. He proposed within twelve months of dating, and they scheduled their wedding date. It was back, that feeling of completion that Mona had in college. Life was happening, and she was finally catching up. Her career was going well, and so was his business. It seemed like they were both at the top of their game. As you can imagine, they felt great to be at such a successful stage in life simultaneously together.

Mona felt like she was living the dream. She did almost everything she set out to do. She'd seen women on social media complaining about guys they would meet online and how it ended up being one huge fail, but that wasn't her story. The icing on the cake was the fact that she didn't have to spend unnecessary time dating all sorts of different men. Instead, she was fortunate enough to meet her guy on the first round and they were actually on the same page.

Within two years, Shawn and Mona were engaged, married, and pregnant. Things were happening fast, but they were happy. Early in the pregnancy, as happens for most expecting parents, they realized that neither one of them quite knew what to expect outside of what friends shared. They stayed up hours at a time planning for Ava's arrival and Shawn was especially excited to be having a girl.

It was at this time that Mona finally convinced her grandma to move out West; not a hard sell, once she heard that Mona was with child. She was packed and on the first flight over. Grandma loved Shawn and he loved her. It didn't take long for her to get acclimated and Mona was so happy she decided to come. Between her hours at the hospital and Shawn's hours at the agency, they were both running around like chickens with their heads cut off. Grandma added calm to the storm.

Time seemed to fly by. It felt like one second Mona was announcing her pregnancy, and then the next, she was scheduling her C-section. Little Ava was already being a little deviant. She refused to turn around. When the doctors saw that she was breached, they scheduled the delivery, not wanting to take any chances. Grandma and Shawn were there every step of the way, holding Mona's hands and rubbing her back. On Monday at 8:30 am, they wheeled her in and within two-hours, she was sleeping off the anesthesia. Ava was fine, grandma was cooing, and Shawn was drowning in love. It was picture perfect, really, but since Mona was cut, she had to stay in the hospital a few extra days.

She enjoyed her stay, but was ready for release day. Grandma pushed Mona to the elevator in a wheelchair since they wanted her to take it easy. Seeing Shawn carry Ava in his arms gave Monat that complete feeling again. When they got to the car, she looked around and saw her family with smiles spread across their faces. The feeling of complete wholeness that Mona felt in that moment simply cannot be described.

The next few months were an adjustment as Mona took a year off from the hospital, and Shawn promoted one of his assistants to manager.

They both decided they wanted to be there as much as possible for Ava's first year. At first, it was great. Both Shawn and Grandma were there to cover night shifts, and they eagerly stepped in when Mona needed a break during the day, which turned out to be quite often. As excited as she was to have Ava and get her home, actually having her there was an entirely different story. When she cried, Mona didn't want to be bothered. Ava would dirty her diaper and Mona would instantly feel overwhelmed. She started sleeping through her cries at night and began not wanting to get out of bed in the morning. Mona didn't know exactly what was going on, she just knew that her completeness was fading and now she was simply feeling overloaded.

Grandma noticed it first, or at least she was the first to say something. "Girl, what's wrong with you? You might need to speak with your doctor. You aren't acting like yourself." Mona blew her off and simply chalked it up to Grandma being overprotective, but then a few weeks later, Shawn said something too. "Mona, you're acting a little weird. Is everything okay?" Mona didn't even respond. Everything annoyed her. She started second guessing everything from being a mother, to being a wife, to even being alive period - it all just seemed to be that overwhelming. She thought she could handle anything, but this was proof that she couldn't. All of her friends looked so happy. They never shared stories about suddenly feeling different. So, where was all of this coming from?

Everyone spent the first year of Ava's life walking on eggshells. Nobody wanted to set Mona off and she didn't want to be bothered. As Ava continued to grow, Mona continued to grow distant. She went back to work as soon as the year hiatus ended. Shawn's company was doing so well, he could afford to continue to pay the manager and still maintain decent profit margins. Grandma was getting older, obviously, and moving a little slower, so Shawn decided it would be best if one of them continued to stay home. In taking stock of the full situation, Mona had a beautiful baby girl, a devoted husband, and a live-in nanny in for a grandmother. Why was she unhappy? Her family tried to support her, but she was a mess. She was avoiding them by working double shifts, so by the time she got home, everyone was usually asleep or heading to school. It was perfect for Mona and whatever she was dealing with, but it was terrible for her family.

Even with all of the blatant signs that things were off, Mona didn't want to believe that something was wrong with her. She had accomplished too much in life for it to be *her* who had this problem. Mona was the one who literally came from nothing, moved across the country, and built a life for herself from scratch. If anyone should be able to handle adversity, it's her; or at least, that's what she kept telling herself as she watched her family ties unravel.

When Ava was two, Grandma died. To honor her wishes, they traveled back to North Carolina to bury her with her parents and siblings. The journey back to California was a difficult one because Mona knew she didn't have her Grandma as a buffer in the house anymore. She and Shawn were barely speaking to one another at this point, and she was sure Ava knew something wasn't right.

Six months later, Shawn told her that either she go to get help, or they were getting a divorce. "You've been pulling away from me for 2.5 years. Either you want me, or you don't." Mona didn't know what to say. He was a part of that picture of completeness. Shawn made Mona feel happy at one point but that feeling had long gone and Mona didn't know the specifics of exactly what went wrong. She just kept thinking to herself, "Such a good man wasted on me."

Mona continued on her destructive path, working as many hours as she could, refusing to talk to anyone, remaining distant from everyone except for her patients. They made her feel whole. They needed her and she knew exactly what to expect from them, unlike what she found one day when she came home. It was early on a Friday morning and Shawn's car was gone, which was strange since it was so early. As Mona unlocked the door, she found the house to be eerily quiet. Nothing made a sound. She tiptoed upstairs to Ava's room, but she wasn't there. She walked into the master bedroom. No Shawn. They should have been in the bed asleep. As panic set in, she ran over to the closet. They were gone and so were their things. Everything was perfectly in place except for them. Looking back on that dreaded day, Mona was certain that that was how she made them feel time and time again. That they were chocolate stains on an all-white rug.

Funny thing is, she didn't even grab her phone to call right away. She was happy to have a few moments to herself. She was still in shock about where she was in life and she needed to allow it all to sink in. She felt boxed in, like she had no options except the one in front of her. For a second, she wished she had her old life back. Before she knew it, morning turned to afternoon and afternoon to night, and there she was. Still sitting there. Stuck.

She never considered the impact that her family situation had on her. Her mother overdosed during Mona's senior year of high school and some man claiming to be her father showed up at the funeral. She never cried. She accepted that her grandmother was, in essence, her true mother. She pretended that Grandma was all she knew.

When Mona finally saw a counselor, she helped her uncover all that had been buried. She learned that she was striving for more and would continue to in an effort to compensate for what she felt she lost or missed out on. Since Mona refused to address her true feelings, nothing would ever be enough. Her life had become a ticking time bomb and now, it finally blew up.

The phone rang, shaking her from her stupor. "You weren't even going to call to see where we were?" Mona held the phone in her hand, waiting for her brain to deliver the response to her lips. Before she could answer, there was a click on the other end. For the first time, she had to accept that her life wasn't complete, and it wasn't because of Shawn, Ava, or her deceased grandmother. It was because of Mona and the cookie cutter lifestyle American Dream she created.

Kim

CHAPTER 8

Let's Go Half On A Baby

Every day, it's the same thing. Kim's alarm blares at 4 a.m. pulling her from sweet slumber and reminding her that she has goals. It doesn't matter how tired she is, she pulls herself out of those sheets, laces up her sneakers, and puts her game face on. It's time to run! Kim's run group meets every day in downtown Clinton. Together, they run out their frustrations, pound the pavement with their determined feet, and sweat away those tempting desserts. It's been this way for about three years, and Kim wouldn't trade it for the world. She was in a good space. She had her friends, the run group, and her Granny. She couldn't ask for anything else. Well, maybe a man but she was in no hurry.

As they cleared mile three, all Kim could think about was the day ahead. Who would she meet today? Kim loved her job at Middleton Bank. She enjoyed meeting new people and how they made her feel. She liked knowing that she was helping her customers in one way or another. It's good to feel appreciated.

By the time she made it back home, she had time enough to cook breakfast, shower, change, and head for the door. Although she didn't have to be to work until 8:00 a.m., she preferred to arrive around 7:30 a.m. She wanted people to know just how serious she was about her career. When Kim pulled into the parking lot, so did Tiffany, and per usual, Tiffany would barely let Kim get out of the car before she started sharing hubby stories. Kim was happy for her, but she was ready to be the star in her own set of stories. As Kim unlocked the door to begin her work day, she smiled. Tiffany was still talking, not realizing that Kim had stopped listening.

It was Friday, which meant that the day would be busy. Even before the bank was opened, people were already lined up to make deposits and cash checks, and it was highly likely that the day would continue at this pace. Kim thrived in this type of environment. She would welcome the next guest, provide small talk so that they felt welcomed, attend to all of their needs, and have them out before the teller beside her could finish counting her money. Kim was good, but she was also shy. Many of her transactions were completed with her eyes glued to her computer screen. It wasn't until she heard this deep voice that she decided to look up.

It was Mr. Henry. She had heard the other tellers gush over him, but she had never really paid him any attention. "I prefer to see the eyes of the person who is handling my money," he half joked. Kim lifted her gaze to meet his. And he was breathtaking. Mr. Henry was tall, dark, and handsome. He wore a tailored suit, a pretty smile, and well-manicured everything. You could tell that he either cared a lot about how he looked or that he had a really good job that cared. Maybe even both! At the end of the transaction, Mr. Henry slid a card across the counter. Kim pulled it to her to see what his request might be, but it wasn't a request at all. Instead, it was his contact information with a little note on the back that read: Call Me! Kim quickly placed the card in her pocket, not wanting any of the other tellers to see what had just taken place. She knew she was too late when she saw her phone light up. Kim didn't even want to pick up because she knew where it was headed.

The day continued and so did Tiffany's speculations about what had happened between Mr. Henry and Kim. "What were you and Mr. Henry talking about? He stood at your counter longer than any other client you've had today!" Tiffany was eager for Kim to share all of the juicy details. Kim answered, "How do you know how long my clients are at my counter, nosey?" Kim and Tiffany both laughed. When Kim got into her car, she couldn't help but think about what happened. As she sat there getting her mind together, a shadow closed in on her left side. *Knock! Knock!*

Mr. Henry's teeth glistened in the moonlight. He looked like he was ready to take pictures for the cover of GQ magazine. Luckily, Kim wasn't startled. As tellers, they are trained to keep an eye on their surroundings at all times. She turned the key in the ignition and rolled the window down. "Good Evening," she said as she continued to look out her front windshield. "Did you learn nothing from me earlier? I like to see the eyes of those handling my money." He smiled. "But, I'm not handling your money now. The bank is closed." Kim nervously responded.

"Let me take you to dinner. You have to eat, right?" Kim's gaze now shifted from the front of the car to Mr. Henry's hands, as he laid them on her door. His hands were nice. Every nail was clipped and cleaned as if he had just left the manicurist's chair. "Sure." Kim whispered, barely making eye contact.

"Then it's settled. We can leave your car here and you can ride with me. I will bring you back after dinner." Mr. Henry said everything so fast,

Kim barely had time to process it all. He pulled on her door and reached for her hand. "And for goodness sake, don't call me Mr. Henry." Kim laughed as she allowed her hand to rest in his. He opened the passenger door for her and she trustingly got out, although she was quite nervous. It had been a while since she'd been on a date and she wasn't sure what to expect. He sat next to her and put on his seatbelt. "You ready?", he asked with a smile as wide as his windshield. Kim nodded, and they drove off.

Mr. Henry took her to one of the city's most exclusive restaurants. So exclusive, that you had to make reservations. Kim wondered how he had time to do that when he literally just asked her to go. Nonetheless, she promised herself that she would have a good time. When they were seated, he ordered everything for her. Kim wasn't used to this. She was used to handling her own affairs and ordering her own food, but it was a nice change to not have to worry about anything. She shook off the bad feeling and relaxed.

By the end of the night, they both had gotten comfortable. He had taken his jacket off and Kim had let her hair down. They shared laughs, stories about their childhood, and goals for the future. When the waiter brought the ticket, Kim felt a little twinge in the pit of her stomach. She wasn't ready to go, but as they say, all good things must come to an end. When Mr. Henry dropped Kim off at her car, he opened the door for her. He told her he had a good time and that he expected to hear from her once she made it home. He pulled her in for a tight embrace. It had been a while since Kim had allowed anyone in her personal space, and she could tell. They both got in their cars and drove away. Later that night after Kim had showered and got ready for bed, she sent Mr. Henry a message letting him know that she was home safe. He told her he would see her soon.

The next several weeks were a page from a book Kim had never read. Every morning she was greeted with motivational calls, just before her run. Every day at noon, he brought her lunch. Every evening, they frequented a new dinner spot. Although she enjoyed her single life, she really could get used to all of the special treatment. Kim told her mother about him, and how well he treated her. She was so excited because now when Tiffany came to work with stories, she had a few of her own. Things were looking up for Kim. It seemed like her life was really falling into place. She was on the promotional track at work, in good health, and she had a budding relationship.

About six months after their first date, Kim was up for promotion. She excitedly shared the good news with Mr. Henry, only to be met with opposition as he relayed his apprehension, saying that she shouldn't take on too much. His rationale was that soon they would be married, and she would have to be at home with their children. This was something they had not discussed. Kim wanted to be married, but she didn't want to give up her career, and she certainly wasn't quite ready for children. She thought long and hard about his words, and decided she wanted to test the waters. She interviewed for the promotion and got the job. Although she and Mr. Henry continued to date, he made it clear that he was not happy. He complained when she had to work late, or if she brought work home, whether mentally or physically. He didn't agree with Kim's decision, but he still treated her well. He still called in the morning, met her for lunch, and spent most nights with her eating dinner. Kim was happy. Her career was going well and so was their relationship. Of course, there were little hiccups every now and then but nothing she couldn't handle.

About a year into their relationship, Kim began to expect a proposal. He was wining and dining her, seemed like that would be the next obvious step. She hinted. He would quickly shut her down. "We need to get to know each other better, live together, maybe even have a child first before making such a huge commitment." Kim didn't want to mess up a good thing so she decided to give a little. They moved in together just after their one-year anniversary. Kim's mother warned her not to sell her house so she reluctantly agreed to rent it out. In Kim's eyes though, she may as well have sold it. The way she figured it, if they moved in together now, they would be married within the year.

Of course, life didn't plan out like that. Anytime Kim brought up marriage, Mr. Henry had a rebuttal. "We've known each other less than two years. Let's just take our time. Things will happen when they're supposed to." His words used to infuriate her, but she didn't doubt him because of all he had done. He showered her with any and everything a woman could want. "Why would he do all of this and not want to marry me?"

Kim and Mr. Henry didn't get married within the year, but Kim did get pregnant. When she looked down at the stick after puking her guts out for three straight days, she knew two things: 1. Life was changing, and 2. She was about to get married. When she shared the news with Mr. Henry, he told her it was time for her to leave her job and prepare the home for their first-born. Kim wasn't entirely onboard with this plan but figured it would be a good idea since it was their first child. Eight months into her pregnancy and nearly three years into their relationship, Kim put in her notice at work. Her peers were sad to see her go, and her grandmother wasn't in agreement with this decision at all, but Kim felt certain that the ring was on the way.

In the same way that her two-week notice came and went, when the baby came, her sanity went. Mr. Henry continued to work as if they didn't have a newborn, he didn't even take paternity leave. Kim felt alone. Having a new baby was stressful. Ariana was her first child, and although her mother supported her, she couldn't jump up and run to her every time she needed a break. Besides, her mother was getting older. Not to mention the fact that she wasn't trying to hear all of the "I told you so" statements since she had been warned.

Kim began to miss the days before Mr. Henry showed up in her line at the bank. The days when all she had to worry about was waking up on time to go run. She rarely ran anymore now. She didn't have the time. Ariana's sleep patterns had not yet adjusted, and Mr. Henry had slowly but surely talked Kim out of running every day. So much had changed since they had gotten together: she no longer had the career that she loved; her new title was "stay at home mom"; there was no time for the run group to help her pound the pavement along with her stress; and to top it all off, she barely had her mother, who was getting older and didn't care too much for Mr. Henry's changes.

Kim was becoming frustrated. She wished that she could be single again. Instead, she was stuck in a relationship with a man who was no closer to marrying her now than he was the day they met. It seemed like he just wanted the comfort of her being there but didn't want the commitment, which she found to be crazy since he was willing to commit to sharing a child. Mr. Henry was content to have the perfect picture with no real ties. Kim continued to bring up marriage and he continued to dismiss her. The first year of Ariana's life was rough. Kim felt like she had been duped. Sure, he put her and her daughter in a beautiful home. They had nice cars to drive and they ate at some of the most highend restaurants, but he rarely wanted Kim to leave the house. He didn't want her hanging with her friends. Mr. Henry wanted her to get rid of everything that made her independent of him, with no real intentions of making Kim his wife.

After waiting four years for Mr. Henry to make a move, Kim got fed up and left. Luckily, Kim did listen to her mother about one thing: she kept her house! One day while Mr. Henry was away at work, she had a moving company come in to pack up her and Ariana's things. By the time he got off work, they were back at her house. Within a few weeks of leaving, she initiated the paperwork for child support and contacted Middleton Bank to see if they had any positions available. Mr. Henry attempted to get her back. He made all kinds of empty promises that she had heard before. "We will get married. I was just a little scared. I wanted us to be ready." This time, Kim wasn't having it. She and Ariana started mapping out life on their terms.

It would be a rough road. Kim was going from being single to a relationship, to now single again with a child. She didn't expect it to be easy, but she was willing to do the work. She had grown tired of Mr. Henry's lies. For the first time in the years they had been together, she saw the red flags for what they were instead of what she wanted them to be.

Natalie

CHAPTER 9

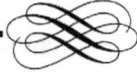

What Natalie Created

Natalie was twenty-six-years-old and tired of working. She'd invested the last ten years of her life to the system as a social worker, her career starting almost immediately after graduating college. Natalie had her eyes set on the position since enrolling her freshman year, and she didn't stop until she made the necessary connections to make that happen. Crazy how something she worked so hard to get beat her down so unapologetically and consistently. Some of the people she worked alongside had lost their zeal, making her job a lot harder. Often times, she found herself not only managing her own case load but also pep talking her coworkers through managing theirs. Natalie understood, somewhat. This job had its way of changing the way you looked at life so it was quite the task to remain positive, especially while removing children from a home for the second time after their mom refused to stick with rehabilitation.

Natalie grew up in the suburbs of Atlanta as the daughter of one of Buckhead's most prominent real estate brokers, Emilyn Highsmith. When you think of strong women, chances are you're thinking of her. She was a hard worker and her success proves how much of a big deal she was. Natalie's friends used to tease her that she wouldn't last long as a social worker, claiming that she wasn't "used to that kind of living". All of the joking only made Natalie want to prove them wrong. Unfortunately, she was starting to believe that they were right about her, but not because of her caseload. No, it was because of her coworkers.

Natalie's friends didn't know that she had her fair share of interactions with "that" side of town. That's where her mother loved to find her men. Ms. Highsmith never really figured love out. She'd been married four times, and each one seemed to be a continuation of the previous relationship, all coming to nothing but dead ends. Due to Emilyn's loveless misfortune, Natalie grew up looking to her mom to be the constant in her life. Her father was never there. He ran off with another woman when Natalie was about eight, and he hadn't looked back since. She and her older sister Naima, were affected by his absence in completely different ways.

Naima had grown to accept it. She figured it meant that her dad wasn't supposed to be in her life, and every man that came in their home only to eventually leave again, was confirmation that we women have to be extremely selective. Her mindset proved to work for her. Naima ended up marrying an anesthesiologist and having two beautiful children. She was happy, undeniably much happier than her mother ever was, or ever would be. Natalie, on the other hand, was scorned. In the few short years that she'd known her dad, she had placed him on a pedestal that soon came crashing down around her. She didn't want to date, and when she did, it seemed like she purposely chose men who weren't good for her. She assumed relationships ended in heartbreak, so she felt no real use in trying.

Ms. Highsmith knew where her estranged husband was, but she never told the girls. She wanted to spare them the heartache. Unfortunately, the secret wasn't hers to keep. Both Natalie and Naima found out that their father had remarried. His new wife had come into the relationship with a couple of children that he started playing daddy for, completely forgetting about the children he had biologically. When they found out in high school, the news took its toll on Natalie. No matter what Naima told her or how much she attempted to reassure her, Natalie had sunken into a dark space as it related to men, specifically her dad.

Natalie decided she wanted to practice abstinence. She figured if she was heartbroken because of a man, then they would be heartbroken because of her with holding the exact thing that she knew they all wanted: sex. She went through high school and college as a virgin. It's likely that many of her relationships were doomed from the moment she shared that she was waiting. Or, maybe they truly were just duds from the start. Between her stale love life and overwhelming work life, Natalie needed a break.

She spent some time with Naima to decompress, and she was wowed at how awesome her life looked. You could feel the love between Naima and her husband. The kids were happy, and so was Naima. Natalie wanted that! She was tired of holding onto what her father had done to their family. It was time to let that go and find some peace of her own. Naima handed her a card before she left her house that day. On the card was a chant, one that Naima had recited so many times before as she found her center and began to really appreciate life. At first, Natalie apprehensively scrunched up her face. Naima quickly jumped in, telling her that it's okay to try something new. because sometimes we need to spend some quality time with ourselves. They both smiled and Natalie left.

The next week she began spending time with herself. She started in the bathroom, seated in front of the mirror. A week into her new habit, and she moved to her spare room. She created a space for herself to chant,

75

meditate, and journal. She began with the intentions of identifying the source of her hurt but soon realized that she had several issues from her childhood buried deep. The more she chanted and meditated, the answers became clearer and clearer on the pages of her journal.

Within six months of starting, she gained so much clarity in her life. She realized it was time to move on from her stressful day-to-day. Natalie was going to quit her job. In the last two weeks at the agency, her coworkers were even nastier. Natalie's manager attempted to load her with more cases, but she knew it would be a bad move since she was leaving. Natalie had never experienced such peace. The calm that she was feeling knowing that part of her life would soon be behind her. When she finally walked out of that door for the last time, she promised herself that she'd never let anyone mistreat her again.

Every night, Natalie would light her candles and prepare to set her intention in the universe through her words. She started tapping into the true depths of her being, all the while she learned to forgive herself for everything she felt she was guilty of, and even decided to forgive her father. Natalie would spend hours writing in her journal, telling the God what she was thankful for. The more she wrote, the more her newfound peace continued to grow.

Natalie's friend, Sheranda, was proud of her for taking the leap. She organized a party to celebrate. Many of Natalie's friends and family were there, as well as a few of Sheranda's associates from the hospital where she was a nurse. One in particular, Caleb - the ER doctor. He was eyeing Natalie all night and she didn't mind, albeit she was a little nervous. From across the room, Sheranda was motioning for her to loosen up. Natalie had reached a really good place and was not ready to take any steps backwards, but she was definitely intrigued. Before the night ended,

Caleb found his way over to her side. No game, no slick lines, just a simple "Hello." They talked for the remainder of the party. He asked for her number before he left and called her the same night. They talked on the phone until the sun came up. The next few months were a dream. They continued to spend time together, and he continued to make her feel like the only girl in the room. Funny thing is, Natalie wrote about love in her journal. She set her intentions for it finding her and it did. Caleb was ten years older than Natalie, and oddly enough had never been married or had any children. He had decided to focus on his career, remaining faith-filled that when he met the one it would be clear to him.

The more they learned about each other, the more intrigued they both became. Naima was proud of Natalie for letting her guards down and trying something new, so she could be prepared for meeting Caleb. Ms. Highsmith was also supportive and invited them all over for dinner and to meet her new mate, who was yet another dud, but Natalie's story was thankfully much different. Within eighteen months of meeting Caleb, they were married, living together, and she was able to dedicate much of her time to working in her community. Natalie ended up creating a nonprofit organization to support those in need. Neither of them were quite ready for children, instead they decided to spend the first year totally immersed in one another. Five years later they were expecting. This was the happiest time of Natalie's life because she was able to really enjoy her life without feeling rushed.

Natalie was grateful for her sister giving her the card with the chant on the back. Naima was the one who got the ball rolling on all of the new changes in her life. Had she not decided to leave her career and focus on her spirituality, she wouldn't have come to terms with all of the issues she had buried. Now that she was free, she could clearly set intentions for her new life. If she would have known that doing so would have had such a major impact on her life, she would have gotten this ball rolling a long time ago. Sometimes it takes hitting rock bottom before you can see the light at the top. Now, Natalie is a mother and a wife living at her best because she chose to create her life. She was smart choosing the man that could make her happy and provide for her and her children. She can't help but to be thankful that she's not where she used to be.

The card Naima gave to Natalie

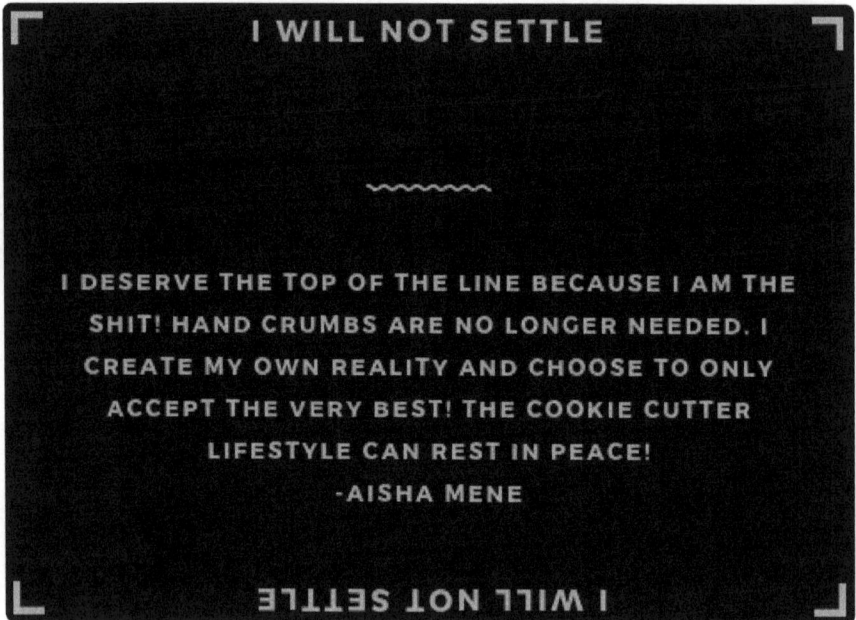

I WILL NOT SETTLE

~~~~~~

I DESERVE THE TOP OF THE LINE BECAUSE I AM THE SHIT! HAND CRUMBS ARE NO LONGER NEEDED. I CREATE MY OWN REALITY AND CHOOSE TO ONLY ACCEPT THE VERY BEST! THE COOKIE CUTTER LIFESTYLE CAN REST IN PEACE!
-AISHA MENE

I WILL NOT SETTLE

(Chant this daily ☺)

Gina Parnell

CHAPTER 10

Ms. Gina Parnell "Ain't Weird"

I adore Gina. She's the ultimate home girl. You know the one whose life you secretly admire? She never had children so she spends her days, and sometimes even months, traveling the world. She sells real estate for a living, and it's not uncommon for her to be gone for months at a time as she scouts new properties. I enjoy being around her because she's so smart. I don't think there's ever been a time where we hung out and I didn't learn something new. Gina was a breath of fresh air. She was a living, breathing, walking manifestation of all of my dreams: a woman with no responsibilities except the ones she set for herself!

Life wasn't always so sweet for Gina, though. When she was sixteen, she saw her sister miscarry in the bathroom of their two-bedroom apartment. She remembers her sister's cries vividly. Not a day goes by where she doesn't recall all of the blood. There was so much blood. The experience scarred her and after it happened, she made up her mind to never have children. Every time I would attempt to ask her about it, she would quickly shut me down with a snippy, "You weren't there!" She was right. I wasn't there. Yet, for some reason, it didn't seem like her sister, Netta, was too traumatized by it all. She continued having children nearly every year after that for the next three years.

Gina hated the life her sister had chosen and she refused to follow in her footsteps. Netta never married any of her children's fathers. Instead, she hopped from one bad relationship to the next. Gina was by her side. She tried to talk her sister into being more careful, but Netta wasn't interested in Gina's philosophies on life. Gina did all she could to help her until one day she realized that she wouldn't be able to change the way Netta saw life. From that moment on, she focused only on herself. Her success. Her freedom. She didn't want the pain, the trauma, or the drama.

I met Gina when she moved to Detroit. I always found it funny that she, a woman who hated the cold so much that she'd go back to Texas for months at a time to escape the cold, would somehow find her way to a city like Detroit; but I was grateful. I looked up to her. She dated quite often, but no guy ever stayed around too long. I never understood that part. Gina took really good care of herself: every day at 5 A.M., she was in the gym and it showed. She was nearly 50 years old, but you couldn't tell. Her hair stayed done, her makeup was always fresh as if she'd just left the MAC counter, and she only wore heels. I think she may even wear them to the gym. Out of all the years I've known her, I've never seen her in flats. She's like wonder woman or something. What was it that kept the guys from committing fully to this powerhouse of a woman? I thought that for years until I realized that Gina played far more of a hand in that than I thought.

Every spring when Gina returned from Texas, she would have a new story about how her parents tried to marry her off. They desperately wanted her to settle down and have a family of her own, but Gina wasn't having it. She had three sisters and each of them had three children. To

Gina, that was enough family.

It's crazy how people only understand from their level of perception. Although Gina's mind was made up about having children, she was still hurt by some of the remarks they made. She couldn't understand why they wouldn't just accept her decision and let her be. On the flip side, her family couldn't understand why she would willingly volunteer for a life of loneliness. What they didn't understand however, was that Gina wasn't lonely. Alone doesn't mean lonely. Quite the contrary, she was fulfilled just as she was. She was happy with her own company and didn't need the validation of others. She loved living out of her suitcase. It made her feel free, like she could go anywhere and be anything that she wanted to be at any given moment.

As for dating, trust me, she was living the life! She had all the men flocking to her, practically bowing at her feet! The difference between her and the rest of us married folk that many single women seem to be jealous of, is that she had the beautiful *option* of the company of men versus the necessity and responsibility of it. Gina was good. She was living her best life, securing the bag, and quick to block anyone who stood between her and her blessings.

Gina is at a level of happiness that I aspire to reach. I call it her American Dream. Although this does not include the husband, children, dog and white picket fence, it does include her own special creation of what works perfectly for her. She brought a new definition to the American Dream in my opinion. For Gina, the American Dream was her manifesting her own desires, not the cookie cutter lifestyle patterned by the expectations of others. Gina, or should I say, Ms. Parnell, is a woman in control of her destiny and anyone who spent even a few minutes with her can tell that her happiness as a result, is truly genuine. Ms. Parnell learned to harness the power of her free will and thus knows that nobody can force her to do anything she doesn't want to do. She is never tied down to anyone she doesn't want to be with. Even though many mothers and wives will never admit it, this is the type of American Dream that many of us envy.

I've overheard people refer to Gina as weird simply because she refuses to conform to society's expectations. I'm here to set the record straight: Gina isn't weird, she's selective! Selective of the places she goes, the people with whom she spends her time, the things that she commits to and the people she allows to commit to her. Gina is protecting her energy, something we all should do. Some may look at Ms. Parnell as weird, but she is a woman who can unequivocally say that she has been in charge of her life every step of the way. She is a shining example of what true womanhood looks like on our own terms.

My Story

CHAPTER 11

Winging It

When I was 24 years old I drove a 2001 Chevy Impala and worked at a hospital as a technical partner. I had my own apartment and I could come and go as I pleased. I never realized how much I enjoyed living there, and yet, I never bought furniture. My place was empty. I didn't get a chance to take it all in and I took that life for granted.

Before living there, I lived in a studio apartment with my boyfriend. He never paid rent, never chipped in to do anything, but for some strange reason, this was the person I chose to be with. Wait, I remember the reason now - it was because I didn't know any better. I didn't know my worth. I was in a bad relationship with someone who didn't love me or treat me how I deserved to be treated. He used me until I couldn't be used anymore. Ladies, never live with a man unless he's paying all your bills and please never give a man money! You work hard enough and you shouldn't be giving your hard-earned money to a man. Let him work and get his own!

Anyway, the apartment was a studio and I hated the smell of it. I even hated to shower there because it had the slide door bathtub which could never be completely clean. I would walk in it every day just to imagine myself in a brand new renovated apartment with ceramic tile, stainless steel stove and fridge, brand new white carpet with drywall. I saw myself in a space reminiscent of the upscale apartments they have in LA. Every day, this is what I would imagine. After a while of living in my studio apartment I got fed up with the smell and the look of it and I began to search for a new place. When I did, there it was online, the exact place I envisioned. Overwhelmed with joy, I just couldn't believe that I was looking at the apartment I'd visualized in my head for so long!

I eventually put my lease up at the studio apartment and stepped into my second apartment, only to be a single woman who was just as unhappy and ungrateful as before.

I took my apartment for granted because I was so worried about a relationship that did not serve me. I stayed too long and did not appreciate the single life I was granted. Each day I cried in my apartment, completely unable to see all of my many blessings. Here I was begging for a man to be with me, instead of moving on and embracing my new place in life.

I never really traveled and I had the wrong friends around me. I had a car full of heels though. All I did was wear heels. However, I entered a new relationship and had my children. I stopped taking care of me. I stopped getting my nails and hair done, and stopped wearing heels too. I just didn't feel I needed to keep myself up anymore because I became "just a mom". Ladies, don't do what I did. Travel, enjoy your life, meet new people, go to new places, and choose to be happy because you deserve it. Don't wing a relationship because you're used to it. Truly indulge in life and enjoy your full purpose!

I started a family consciously, and I use the word "consciously" quite loosely, since in reality, I had no idea what I was doing. As I think back on my feelings for my kid's father, who was only my boyfriend at that time, I can now say that I wasn't fulfilled. I knew I was missing something even then, but I was too immature to know what it was. Our relationship continued, and I allowed myself to get deeper in it because he knew what he wanted, so I was following his lead, even though I didn't know what I wanted. Actually, it would be more accurate to say that I forgot that what I wanted was still important. During my single life, I was living day to day without any real expectations. I came and went as I pleased, not realizing that those precious moments of freedom were slipping through my fingers.

Before I knew it, I was pregnant, and of course, I couldn't get pregnant like normal person, I had to get pregnant with twins! I was supposed to be happy but I wasn't. I was stressed. I knew deep down that I had messed up. The decision to have a child is an intimate one, and it should be among the best moments of a woman's life. Unfortunately, I didn't experience that. My pregnancy was overshadowed with uncertainty, concern, and downright depression. I remember it so clearly, sitting on the couch thinking that my life was over, that this must be it. I cried constantly. Joy was a foreign feeling for me as I headed down this road, internally kicking and screaming. Of course, I don't regret having my children, but I can admit that I wasn't ready.

It was kind of like I had sentenced myself to death, and with that sentence came the need to blame someone. I started thinking about all the things I had never done and instantly became angry. Why was I here? A few signs pointed to my boyfriend. He was the reason I was in this predicament. Then my mind drifted to my mother for not teaching me the order of life. I blamed my dad for not being in my life. I blamed anyone and everyone I could, everyone except for myself.

In my haste to regain some of my freedom, I signed my lease for my old apartment again. As I was preparing to move back in, the landlord pointed out that I needed two bedrooms. Then it hit me, I also needed two cribs. Can you imagine how hard it was going from having no children to having two? It also hit me that I felt stuck in this "situationship". There were so many layers to our relationship and quite frankly, several red flags. It started with an incident that changed the way I saw a few of my friends and ultimately the way I came to perceive him. Before I found out I was pregnant, I looked at my friends who had become parents and relished in the fact that I wasn't one. I felt invincible like it couldn't happen to me. Then it did. As for my man, he wasn't typically an abusive person, but it only takes one time, right? After that one time happened, I was done, or so I thought. Although I no longer liked him, I felt I had to be with him because of our children. So, I stayed.

When I was single and without responsibility, I had no goals or intentions for my life. Then I was in a relationship expecting two children, and I just wanted to escape. Actually, I wanted to overcome, but I didn't know where to start. I was depressed, bitter, and angry, and it didn't help that I couldn't stop reminiscing about how good I used to have it. The thoughts were breaking me down. The more I visualized myself in the past, the more I seemed to lose myself in the present. People who know me well can attest to my positive nature, but when the reality that I was having two children sank in, it was too much. I wasn't able to just shake it off like I had done so many other times before. I didn't want this new life.

Despite it all, I still became a good mother. As much as I wanted to escape, I couldn't leave my babies. It just wasn't in my nature. As my children grew, so did my contentment. With time, I began to accept the decisions I'd made. I knew I couldn't live in this negative mental space forever and I was tired of feeling miserable, so I started putting forth effort with my children's father. Yet, even with effort it seemed like an uphill battle. I held so much resentment towards him, in large part, because I resented myself.

The logical next step for us was marriage, right? At least, that's what he was thinking and apparently, I outwardly agreed. When he proposed to me, I said yes despite knowing that getting married wasn't what I wanted. There was a time when I wished things had happened in their proper order, you know: date, relationship, marriage, then kids. I felt like we were already married. We had done so many things that married people do already. I felt trapped. I thought if things would have happened the right way, he wouldn't have had the pressure of children to motivate his proposal. Love would have done that. Moreover, I wouldn't have the pressure from the children to say yes. Love would have directed me too. I wanted to date, travel more, and come home to a quiet place without anyone asking me to do anything. I was tired of being needed. I just wanted to be free again. I wanted to go out without people asking me how the kids were. It was just hard.

Twins are no joke. I went from having zero to two children. Of course, I felt as though I had to be with him! I couldn't run away from my children and I knew that I certainly couldn't do it alone. To his credit, my kids' father, being the man that he was, would have never let me do it alone either. However, after our last child, my daughter, came into the world, I decided to make up my mind and do what was best for me.

Now I don't want to come off painting my kids father as a bad guy. He's actually a beautiful person inside and out. There really weren't many issues...except for the fact that I was no longer in love. I tried for years

91

but it only became harder after a while. I don't understand why we feel obligated to stay because of the children. Many of my family members told me to work it out however; I came to realize that after ten years of our relationship I ran out of gas. Throughout the years that I was unhappy, I would ask people to help me figure out if he was the person I should be with. Many people looked at my life as a blessing because I had everything a woman could want. I possessed a great house, nice car, beautiful children, and a good man and father that supported me and provided for all of our needs. Some of my friends thought I was crazy to feel the way I did because they themselves longed for a man who treated them and their children the same way my kids father did. However, they never understood that I was not happy. How could they understand? I had "everything".

Yeah, I searched for the answers from everyone, but rarely did I ever stop to search for the answer within myself. When I assessed why I was scared to leave, I found that it was because I knew many people would tell me that I would never find a man as good as him. They'd say that men are horrible and it's hard to find a good man. Little did they know, I wasn't interested in looking for a new relationship, instead, I was looking forward to my new single life. I wanted to go back and appreciate all of the little things that I forgot to be thankful for along the way.

Ladies it's very hard maintaining a relationship when you are simply unhappy. Staying becomes easier said than done. A saying that I will always take with me is to never take advice from a person who you don't want to trade places with. This one statement clarifies my situation so well! Yes, my kids' father is beautiful inside and out, however, things just didn't work out. Sometimes it's best to move on rather than to waste years of your life with someone who is not for you.

A lot of people will never walk away from unfruitful relationships due to their fear of the unknown. Hell, most will never admit that they are unhappy because they want to keep up the perception that they have a perfect life. Why do we torture ourselves this way? What makes our heads decide to stay when our hearts know that we should have left a long time ago? We should know when to walk away. I didn't want to be that girl anymore. I had to be brave enough to walk away, even if I left with nothing. In leaving, it seemed like I was risking it all, yet risk it all, I did.

Never stay too long in a relationship that no longer serves you! Take it from me, a woman that stayed with a man for 10 years all for the children's sake and because I overly valued what others thought of me. Before stepping into a long-term relationship with a man that may not be for you, take the time to think and make a wise and prudent decision.

I can never turn back the hands of time and it sometimes hurts me to look back and see all of the wasted years. I used to feel as though I was a young 26-year-old living in a 30-year-old body. It kind of reminds me of people who have gone to jail for several years and finally are getting out. Their bodies have aged, but in many ways, their minds haven't. Yet, I can't say that nothing good has come out of all of it. I do feel as though I have learned a lot throughout my life. I no longer will accept any and everything anymore. I know now what I didn't know then. I don't want mediocre relationships because I now expect more. I am no longer "just winging it" when it comes to this relationship thing. I am stepping out on faith and along the way I am finding my individuality while simultaneously teaching my children not to make the same mistakes I did.

Through that, I now have a passion to not just teach my kids, but also give single women a blueprint of my life so they no longer have to unwittingly walk in the wrong direction. Just picture me as the woman who has done everything wrong for you. Hey, I'm advocating for you. Just refer to me as the Single Woman's Advocate! Now, there is no need for mistakes. If you ever find yourself being in an unfulfilled relationship leave, especially while you don't have children. Not to be too blunt but children do complicate situations. Don't be that girl, run now while you still have a chance. You can turn your singleness into being fulfilled forever by putting you first and living the most beautiful life you can. Ladies you can do this!

Be the single girl who does whatever she wants when she wants to. Be excellent, stylish, loving, and be fulfilled in every place of your life. Never base your life off of a man. Put you first and you will be at your best. Ladies learn that you are God's gift to the world. Once you realize that you are the prize you will no longer accept anything less than what you truly deserve. Now, I have smelled the coffee and I realize that I am the director of my future. I no longer choose to wing a friendship, relationship or my life. I am now living it to the fullest.

CHAPTER 12

———— ❧ ————

Live Your Own American Dream...

When we hear the words "American Dream," our minds tend to drift to rather similar imaginations. In our pursuit of this pre-constructed dream, we do what we feel is best based on where we are in life. However, what if I told you that the American Dream isn't reality. Saying that it is a reality, only gives life to the narrative that this dream only looks like one thing, but it doesn't. Indeed, the American Dream is whatever *you* want it to be!

I've been there. Too many times, I've found myself in the chapters of the women above. I wanted to live my life, but was wholly unaware of what that meant. The truth is, I was never taught about relationships, nor was I shown how to love myself.

When I started this book, I did so with the intention of telling women to take caution when having children. I wanted women to know that parenting isn't easy, and it isn't something you should go into lightly. As I shared each story, I discovered a deeper message: women must take caution in how they relate to others and even more importantly, to themselves!I realized that having children wasn't the problem, having children when our mental health isn't solid or having children in an unhealthy situation is the real problem.

This process has been enlightening for me, and it has ignited within me a passion to empower women to love themselves so unapologetically that they'd rather be single and whole than be in a relationship and broken. Imagine the impact on our children's lives if we became more discerning with the process of how we enter relationships, gave more thought to choosing who we have sex with and ultimately who we spend our lives with. The impact would be significant.

Many of us are simply trying to figure it all out. If no one else is willing to say it, I will, what we have as women, is too precious to figure out! The unfortunate thing is that many of us are brought up in what society deems as a broken home, and in those cases, we aren't able to see what healthy relationships look like because our mothers are like us, in that, they are figuring it out too. In the end, we are left to draw our own misguided conclusions of what love really looks like.

Take my life story from this chapter and see it not as a tragedy, but as a testimony. I want women to know that they don't have to follow in my footsteps, or in the steps of the other women named. You can do better. Don't live *the* American Dream. Instead, live *you're* American Dream! Live the life you want, devoid of the unhealthy pressures of others. Had I not made the decision to live my purpose, I would have never had the courage to start my business or even write this book! When you rely on people too long, it starts to eat away at your power. We all have power and purpose, we just have to tap into it.

Remember, there's no rush into beginning relationships that will blossom into marriages that produce a household full of children. Trust me, there will be time for that if that is even what you want at all! I say that we need to spend a little more time with ourselves! Relationships take a lot of work, no matter how simple others make them seem. Raising children is also life changing, and they both come with a great deal of responsibility. Handle yourself first before adding more into your life. Let's be about the business of learning to love *ourselves* more, giving *ourselves* the space to blossom, and exploring our purposes. Some of our timelines for self-discovery will be longer than others, and that's okay... live *your* "American Dream".

CHAPTER 13

I Am Your Single Women Advocate

This book is my gift to the world. Let it be a highlighter over the messages in our lives that need revisiting. Use it as a magnifying glass to the issues that we so often overlook. We need to love ourselves more, build better friendships, and take care in how and who we date. If you're like me, then you didn't have a blueprint mapped out for you while you were growing up. In that case, I am talking to you. Better yet, we are talking to each other.

Many times, the mistakes we make in relationships and the red flags that we overlook, are a direct result of not knowing better. How does that old saying go? "When you know better, you do better!" Unfortunately, a lot of us didn't know better. The common theme among most of the women in this book was broken homes, absent fathers, and shaky relationships with mothers. It's a cycle, and a vicious one at that. Hurt women starting families with men who are not ready to be father figures, is a recipe for disaster. When the father leaves, he leaves holes in nearly everything he's left behind. The mother feels the void because now she's raising children alone. Her daughters may look for a father figure in other men. In so doing, she may make herself vulnerable to men who won't

99

have her best interests at heart. Likewise, her son may desert women, showing little regard to their feelings, and making his mother and other women a target for misplaced blame. If the brokenness isn't addressed, ultimately, the cycle continues.

As I said, when you know better you do better, and that's one of my goals with this book. I want to show you some possible outcomes of what happens when you enter relationships haphazardly, but moreover, I want to relay ways in which you can avoid that pitfall. I want to shed light on the work we all have to do within ourselves before we can healthily move forward in our relationships. I am going to give you some tangible next steps to begin living the life that you want to live. However, it must be said that after you finish reading the next section, you can no longer say that you don't know better. Once you know better...well, you know what comes next. Are you ready?

Self-Love

Before you dive into this section, I want you to ask yourself "what does self-love mean to me?" I also want you to identify what you do specifically that is a reflection of you loving yourself. There is a need to discuss self-love for many reasons. People all over the world are making money off of it with books, counseling, apparel, and journaling, so we can conclude that the topic is still relevant. The women's stories shared in this book are reflections of what it looks like to not love yourself enough.

Take Candace for example. She had a baby by Jerry, a man of convenience who lived down the street. I understand that, as women, we want to have fun and date around, however, if your fun is going to have negative implications on your life then perhaps you need to rethink what your meaning of "fun" is. Men show us who they are without us having to ask them. Their actions will provide an indication for how they feel about us and their level of respect for us. If you see his true colors and continue to put your life on the line, then you're showing a lack of self-love. Putting your life on the line is having unprotected sex with a man who isn't responsible. It is also continuing to engage with a man who does not share your relationship goals. Instead of proceeding into a situationship, choose self-love and keep it moving.

Victoria's story had different details but the same root of the lack of self-love. She didn't love herself enough to know that her life was great just the way it was! She envied another woman, which can be a slippery slope. The parts of people's lives that we see isn't always reflective of the entire truth. In this case, Victoria's friend told her the truth but she was so enamored that she ignored all of the warnings. Women are strong-willed. When we set our sights on something, we won't stop until we get it and, unfortunately, we are not exempt from the mistakes that come as a result. She saw that her friend had something she wanted. There is nothing wrong with wanting a family, however, we must check ourselves to ensure we are in the right space for such a great responsibility.

You may wonder, "What is the right space?" The right space is one that is clear. Do you love yourself enough to get clarity and truth on where you are in life? Are you committed enough to yourself to not only pray for clarity, but also act when things become clear? You have to love yourself more than your wants, and when you do, you will see a shift in your focus. You won't tolerate mistreatment because you will be clear on what mistreatment is. Self-love isn't a trend, it's a necessity. Until you realize that, you will continue to allow things into your life that aren't good for you. Don't make excuses for others to mistreat you, and don't mistreat yourself. You only get one you, so fall in love for the long haul.

My mother used to say, you'll be happy if you have one friend. Growing up, I didn't quite understand. It wasn't until I got older that it began to make more sense. Your friends will either make you or break you, so when you're taking a look around, you are literally looking into a mirror. Our friends have so much influence on us, just like we have an influence on them.

Sheila, for instance, didn't realize that Jessica wasn't her friend until it was too late. The night they were in the club and Sheila got wasted, Jessica should have made sure she got home safely. When you're close with someone, you know what type of person they are. If you know your friend isn't a "sex on the first date" kind of person, why allow them to leave with someone when they're clearly inebriated? That was the first red flag, and although there were many others, two in particular come to mind: when Jessica told Sheila to ignore her gut, and when she was excited about the news of pregnancy while Sheila was in turmoil. In my experience, a woman's intuition is typically spot on. We just know when something isn't right. The fact that her "friend" made her second guess what she was feeling, assisting Sheila in weakening her sense of self, is a sign that she wasn't in support of her best interest and was instead, part of the problem. As far as the pregnancy went, sure, babies are exciting but when your friend is breaking down, that may not be the time to celebrate. Essentially, we have to be careful of how we enter into relationships. That isn't just with romantic relationships, but also with those that we call friends.

After you've learned to love yourself, and gotten clear on who your friends really are, then it's time to take a look at dating and how you should proceed into it. I want you to explore your options and understand that you don't have to settle for just any or everybody. You don't need a baby to define your relationship, so be careful with your body. You need to understand your purpose in life and know that if you don't like something you, and only you, have the ability to change it.

There is such a thing as a good man. They are out there bettering themselves every day. They are saving for the future and preparing themselves to be the head of their household. Men should be providers. Any man that wants to have a baby but lacks financial stability should not be in a sexual relationship. This goes for women too. If either party chooses to be intimate knowing they are incapable of parenting, they should protect themselves and each other by wearing contraceptives.

A child should be brought up in a happy home where two parents are financially, mentally, and physically prepared to provide. As a woman who has experienced a life where I had low self-esteem, I remember it giving me a feeling that my life was over. I felt that I had lost a game that I could never play again, but it doesn't have to be this way for you. I want you to love yourself and be certain of where you're headed. If you're single, wear that badge with pride and be secure in who you are. Don't let a man or woman throw you off track. Otherwise, you'll end up like the characters in this book. You can live your best life just as you are, but you have to take control. You must choose against making poor decisions. Don't settle. *Don't Be That Girl!*

Instead, be the girl who steps out on faith believing that there's more to life than just existing. There's greater triumph to be experienced than just making it day to day. There are a plethora of opportunities that open themselves up to you when the decision is made to leave people that no longer serve you. Understand that you are not walking in abundance, you are walking abundance, so you don't have to be afraid to be alone. Learn yourself. Once you do, you'll serve a much higher purpose. You are amazing and I believe in you! Take it from me, your Single Woman Advocate!

I would love for you to connect with me!

single_women_advocate_

SINCEWEREHERE LETSTALK

www.ingramcontent.com/pod-product-compliance
Lightning Source LLC
Chambersburg PA
CBHW060031050426
42448CB00012B/2952